# Thoreau's Backyard

## Musings from a Small Town

### Glenn Rifkin

*Best Wishes,*

**Windingwood Press**

Also by
Glenn Rifkin

———————————

*The Ultimate Entrepreneur: The Story of Ken Olsen and Digital Equipment Corporation* (with George Harrar)

*Radical Marketing: From Harvard to Harley: Lessons From Ten Who Broke the Rules and Made It Big* (with Sam Hill)

*The CEO Chronicles* (with Douglas Matthews)

*Radical E* (with Joel Kurtzman)

*A Thousand Tribes* (with Robin Lissack and George Bailey)

*The CEO and the Monk: One Company's Journey to Profit and Purpose* (with Robert Catell and Kenny Moore)

*MBA In A Box* (with Joel Kurtzman)

Thoreau's Backyard; Musings from a Small Town

Copyright © 2004 by Glenn Rifkin

Windingwood Press, Publisher

5 Windingwood Lane
Acton, MA 01740
978-635-3451

ISBN 0-9762453-0-2

To my Janie, who is the light around my heart;

To Cameron, Laura, Ben and Sunny,
my North, my South, my East, my West;

And to Lillian, our leading lady.

# *Introduction*

In the autumn of 1996, I decided to get on my bicycle and pedal 300 miles from Boston to New York City. In the aftermath of some personal emotional trauma, I figured that doing something physically demanding would be a great distraction so I signed up for the Boston-New York AIDS Ride. I was right. The ride was daunting, exhausting, draining but also exhilarating and affirming in ways I hadn't expected.

Being a writer, when I returned from the ride I took pen to paper (or fingers to keyboard as it were) to chronicle my experience. I sent the finished essay to The New York Times and later the Boston Globe, but both rejected it. So on a lark, I emailed the piece to Lucille Daniel, the editor of the Concord Journal, my dulcet hometown newspaper which arrived every Thursday in my mailbox. Lucille immediately responded saying she would love to run the story and asked for photos to accompany it. She also asked me if I would be interested in contributing regularly to the Journal.

Given that I received the princely sum of $45 for my article, I promptly declined. As a professional journalist writing for The New York Times and other big time publications, I reasoned that the Journal couldn't afford me and I couldn't afford it. But when my article appeared, something interesting happened. I got immediate and wonderful reaction from people in Concord, my neighbors, acquaintances, and strangers I'd meet in Concord Teacakes or the Cheese Shop or Debra's Natural Gourmet. I had an epiphany. A byline in The New York Times that reaches millions of readers around the world is not necessarily any more personally fulfilling than a byline that touches the community around you. In fact, an argument could be made that writing for a small, local audience, an audience you could come to know on a first-name basis, might be even more satisfying and exhilarating.

I got back to Lucille with an offer: I will contribute a column to the Journal for its op-ed page, but it must be published as I wrote it, and I get to choose the headline as well. I could write about whatever I wanted (within the bounds of good taste) and contribute whenever the mood moved me. Somehow able to see past my prima donna attitude, Lucille decided to give it a shot. And thus began a long and fruitful relationship with the Concord Journal. I called the column Making Contact, and I began to turn out these personal essays on a monthly basis.

I wrote about a wide array of topics, from watching my young son learn to ice skate to a wonderful "walking lady" whose name I never knew but who touched me with her very presence. I observed world events and how they played on the green streets of our town. I wrote about people in town and about the town of Concord itself, which tapped a special spot in my heart during the five years I lived there. I continued to write even when Lucille, much to my regret, decided to leave the paper. I have worked with a string of editors in her place over the years, all wonderful and dedicated and vastly underpaid, and the formula has not changed at all. Even when I moved from Concord to Acton and thought my column days were finished, I was asked to keep writing. My life, in most important ways, continued to center on Concord anyway, and I figured I was just a mile from the town border so my musings remained valid, if not geographically perfect.

And even when the Journal, along with its sister CNC publications, was sold to the Boston Herald and budgets were cut so that I no longer got paid for my column, I continued to write. I hadn't been in this for the money anyway. I had something to say and readers who seemed to care enough to read my words and let me know they were moved by them in some way.

And that really was the heart of the matter. In this remarkable town, where Thoreau, Hawthorne, Emerson, Louisa May Alcott and so many others had used the written word to magically transform the world, I had this wonderful opportunity to touch people's lives, and in many ways this became more fulfilling to me than any of the articles I wrote or books that I published. I had, in effect, made contact, and that was worth more than money.

So when my great friend David Stark, the talented brother of Debra Stark of Natural Gourmet fame, suggested I put some of my columns into a collection and offer it out to the world, I was intrigued. After stalling and procrastinating for a long time, I thought, Why not? Maybe this will strike a chord or touch a heart or become a gift to someone in the same way it has been a gift for me.

So without further explanation, I offer this collection to the people of Concord and people in small towns everywhere. I doubt that anyone will get the same pleasure reading these as I had writing them, but if it comes close, it will be well worth the effort.

Glenn Rifkin
Acton, Massachusetts
September, 2004

# Winter

In the corner of Hawthorne Village, the plow created a mountain of snow, which to the five-year olds rose up like Everest. As long as the icy cold kept it intact, there was, for days, the sound of squealing delight and snowpants sliding down the glacier. I could only bribe them in with the promise of hot chocolate and cookies and when they arrived in the hallway, puffs of cold breath and cheeks the color of stoplights, it was many minutes of grunting and tugging to remove snow-covered boots and drenched parkas. In those moments, the winter was no longer the endless season of lightless days but the purveyor of memories already coalescing, already signaling a special passage. ❏

# The Skating Lesson

It is a cold February Saturday morning, and I am standing near the ice at a local rink in town. The cold inside the rink is deeper, more bone chilling than outside, a feeling of being inside a refrigerator or giant freezer.

Out on the ice, pandemonium reigns. An army of tiny skaters inhabits the rink, slip-sliding around the ice like a flock of arctic penguins playing on a giant ice flow. This is the Learn to Skate program sponsored by my town's Youth Hockey Association. From January to the end of March, this becomes my Saturday morning ritual, a regular hour of frostbitten fatherhood that I wouldn't trade for a thousand easy chairs and a roaring fire.

Out there on the glassy white surface, somewhere among the penguins, is my seven-year old, Benjamin, virtually anonymous in an oversized hockey helmet, jersey, and snow pants. But like a mother bat finding her baby in among a million upside-down cave dwellers, I can spot Ben quickly. Okay, he is wearing number 22, and his snow pants have a distinct green stripe on the legs. But I'd find him anyway. I know this child, believe me.

For I've entered an era here, a slope of years in which there is no second chance and no going back. This is T-ball time, and soccer mornings and the chance to watch a child stumble and fumble around the ice, falling, sprawling, searching me out with a look of dismay and betrayal that I sent him out there where the surface is slick and he is bound to fall.

Outside the glass, I have stood now for two winters and fought off the distinct urge to walk out on the ice to lift him back up and give him his balance. It really hasn't been that tough, not so much because of my own willpower but because of his. Benjamin gets back up. He always has. Like all the other five-year olds and six-year olds and seven-year olds swarming around him. Children are constantly teaching us about resilience and second chances.

A coach, some overweight father who skates like hell and is big as a bear but gentle and caring, checks them out if they fall. But he doesn't pick them up either. He points to the other end of the rink and sends them off again, wobbly legs searching for balance.

And the reason I tend not to leave the rink and hide in the warmth of the coffeeshop is that I've never wanted to miss that one moment when Benjamin finally gets it, when the disjointed pieces of this slick mystery all come together and he skates. At first, he was bent and sort of hobbling, an elderly man making a slow journey to a park bench.

Ben would skate/walk to the glass where I stood, and he'd smile at me through the cage on the helmet. "Did you see how fast I was going?" he'd ask me, beaming as if he'd just won gold at Lillehammer. I had to read his lips because I couldn't hear him through the glass. I would give him the thumbs up sign we shared and off he'd go, once around again.

The other moms and dads stake out similar posts, sharing my vantage point and spotting their own with eagle eyes and the same deep love that we feel for these children. We chat and share war stories about the flu that is going around and the impossibility of getting plane tickets to Florida during school break. We make contact at the edge of our children's lives and then rush off to gather them up when they stagger off the ice, cheeks red with the cold and the exertion.

Benjamin smiles at me as we tromp into the crowded and noisy locker room to start the ritual delayering of gear. "Good job, buddy!" I tell him as we high five and start untying his skates.

When we leave the rink, a bag of chips clutched in his hands and me schlepping his gloves, hat and equipment bag, I glance down at him and remind myself how far this tiny person has to go. We talk about his newfound command of this ice, about the way it feels so great to know that you've learned something that will stick with you for a lifetime.

And it is just another skating lesson, I remind myself. But as I slip the key into the ignition, I look over at this child who has become my best friend in what seems like the blink of an eye, and realize that I'd been heading to this rink, on this Saturday morning, for just this reason, all of my life. ❑

# A Hanukkah Story

In 1979, as a young writer for the Boston Phoenix, I was asked by my editor to do the obligatory Hanukkah story. Amid the crush of Christmas coverage, publications would inevitably run one or two Hanukkah pieces to appear politically correct and not offend the Jewish readership. It was mostly a silly sham, a gesture to a holiday that seemed to me as a Jewish boy growing up in a Christian community in New Jersey, a poor cousin to the wonders of Christmas.

Hanukkah was a joyous celebration, no doubt. I loved lighting the candles on the Menorah, opening presents, spinning the dreidel. But all this paled in comparison to what was happening at my friends' houses where there were Christmas trees, carols on the record player, stockings on the mantelpieces and mountains of presents that seemed to climb to the ceiling. Hanukkah was fun but Christmas was magic.

While some Jews grew to be offended by the excesses of Christmas and its crass commercial stranglehold on our society, I fell in love with the holiday from afar and secretly wished that I could somehow find a way to celebrate it as my friends did. It was nice to enjoy the carols on the radio and classic Christmas movies on television, but it just wasn't the same as being there.

And that winter in 1979, not long after my father had died, I was empty and sad and feeling as if the impending holiday season would just swallow me up like a small boat in a big wave. I was in no mood to write about recipes for potato pancakes or innovative Menorahs. Instead, I found a small Hanukkah miracle of my own. I had heard that Elie Wiesel, the noted author and Holocaust survivor, had begun teaching at Boston University. What, I wondered, did Hanukkah mean to him? Perhaps there would be a story there.

When I called, Wiesel, a soft-spoken and gracious man, invited me to come to his office at BU. I was taken by this slightly-built man with eyes that bespoke the deepest sadness and the most profound wisdom. When he spoke, I had to lean forward to hear each word. And he told me this story:

It was December, 1944 in the dark cold of the Auschwitz death camp. There, a small group of Jews did the unthinkable: they celebrated Hanukkah. Weisel was a 16-year old boy from the Transylvanian village of Sighet. He remembers vividly how a close friend somehow got hold of some potatoes and a small bit of oil. "It defied every logic, every safety measure or possibility," Weisel recalled. "But very secretly, we lit those candles and said the prayers." Had they been caught, they would have been killed on the spot. It was an act of hope in the midst of desperation, a desire to embrace life in a place of death and observe the holiday against all odds.

Weisel somehow survived Auschwitz and Buchenwald and has spent a lifetime since writing and lecturing about the Holocaust, teaching religion and philosophy, championing causes for world peace, and coming to grips with being Jewish in a hostile world. He has won the Nobel Peace Prize and become an advisor to presidents. And he has never forgotten that one special Hanukkah.

In fact, Wiesel had a childhood of wonderful Hanukkah memories, growing up in Romania as the dark pulse of fascism grew stronger around him and his family. "Hanukkah was so totally different," he said. "It was communication, it was friendship, it was visiting. The stories we heard, the beautiful stories about Judah the Maccabee; for a child in a small town in Eastern Europe surrounded with fear, it was important to know that a man named Judah the Maccabee was his ancestor."

Unlike the assimilation of Jews into American society, Wiesel's life was clearly marked, a community ostracized, separated and abhorred by those around them. They found their comfort and joy by embracing their heritage. "Every holiday was important. Especially this one that lasted so long," Wiesel recalled. "We got one gift, a few pennies for Hanukkah gelt. There was something to looking at the candles. I loved that. To watch them grow one more and one more. The ceremony of lighting the candles was very beautiful, very touching."

Wiesel could not comprehend the idea that Hanukkah had evolved in America as a weak imitation of Christmas, an excuse to include Jewish children in the holiday season. "We never took cues from the Christian world," he told me. "For us, Hanukkah was a genuine tradition that we inherited from century to century.

We looked forward to Hanukkah just like we looked forward to the High Holy Days."

I wrote this story for the Boston Phoenix and it remains one of my favorites after 18 years and more articles than I can count. It changed Hanukkah for me forever. I still love Christmas and its twinkling lights. But now, when Hanukkah comes, it calls up an image of this small group of Jews, lighting a light in the darkest night. In a season of miracles, it is the one I remember. ❏

# The Problem with Love...

I was born on Valentine's Day. While this has never qualified me as the Love Doctor, it does give me certain Cupidistic qualities. A year and a half ago, for example, I invited two good friends to join me on a bicycle ride up Monument Street and into Great Brook Farm State Park in Carlisle. Let's just say that by the time I reached Lowell Road on the way home, these two were four miles back, deep in conversation and pedaling just fast enough to keep their bikes from toppling over with inertia. When they finally arrived back at Monument Square, they'd arranged a first date and they remain in love to this very day.

Love, of course, is a splendid thing and I've always believed that because of my unusual birthday, I've had just a smidge more feel for this strange and wondrous emotion than others. I've been writing poetry, for example, since I was 12, and though Dickinson and Keats have little to fear, I've turned a sonnet or two in my time. I've felt love, seen love, made love, found love, lost love, fought for love, run from love, embraced love.....I've been all over love, believe me.

The problem with love, it seems to me after all these years, is that it has this unfailing propensity to beget relationships. And that is where the whole concept turns strange and incoherent, where the blue sky of pure unfettered joy gets clouded over with dark menacing storms of human frailty and insecurity. It is, it seems, like the shuttle bus that arrives at the Caribbean resort to transport you to the airport and back to reality,

Relationships, in effect, are the by-product of love but often have very little to actually do with love. "Love is a sickness full of woes..." wrote the poet Samuel Daniel. And that was in the 16th century. Obviously, little has changed in this department. Human beings, propelled by exploding synapses and gallons of weird brain chemicals, are quite helpless to avoid this odd two-step, but the whole tango seems bizarre to me because it is right there in our faces all the time. Short of movies, all people seem to talk about are relationships—how impossible they are; how much we want one.

This powerful point of embarkation, where love becomes relationship, has become nothing less than an industry in our beleaguered country. Indeed, there is an entire industry for finding each other, and yet another for what to do once we've become hopelessly lost in the morass of each other. One industrious author with a clever head for jingles came up with "Men are from Mars, Women are from Venus" and with that he has ensured that generations of his heirs will never have to hold meaningful jobs. The single phrase spawned not only countless book sequels, but seminars, videos, and now even a monthly magazine.

He, like thousands of others, found this sweet spot, the confounding duality of love, and panned it for gold, like modern-day Forty-Niners converging on California. And we, as a society, don't begrudge these harbingers of hope their shiny cars and tax deductions because we want answers, we crave answers to an unsolvable dilemma.

My bicycle friends are still in love, for example, but one would need a scorecard and date book to track whether or not they are still together on any given day. Sometimes they themselves don't even know.

And they are hardly unusual. Making the transition from love into harmony is a bit like arriving from Akron and driving through downtown Boston for the first time. You might not get hopelessly lost in a maze of one-way streets, road construction and dead ends, but it's not likely. Despite the volumes of advice, there are no road maps for love, and the highway is littered with your friends and mine, dazed, confused, driving off slowly while muttering to themselves.

But don't despair. Love, the most powerful of emotions, spawns a whole subset of feelings, including hope. The divorce rate is suddenly dropping, baby boomers are more than ever committed to their partners, willing to stick it out because, many believe, the upside of alone is much worse than the downside of together.

Besides, I was born on Valentine's Day, the offspring of romance. As Carly Simon wrote, "I believe in love, what else can I do..?" And that's it exactly. What else can we do? We are helpless to these strange, enticing rhythms, so we may as well turn up the music and dance.  ❏

# Following the Dog to a Path
## Less Traveled

We know these woods, Sunny and I. The past 18 months, we have hiked these paths that spread like spider webs through the pine and maple and oak. We no longer watch the seasons from a distant window, we walk them day after day under the canopy of trees and sky.

It is only 18 months and she is still, by any stretch, a puppy. But these woods now feel like a lifetime haven where the stillness touches you as you walk. You don't hear the quiet until you stop, until you cease the crunching of leaves or snow under your boots. Sunny always stops with me, listening, searching the distance with expectation. Though we have never seen anything but small birds or a chevron of Canadian Geese overhead, we know the animals in these woods. We see the beds of pine needles where the deer lie at night. We notice the distinctive beaver markings where the felled trees lie down near Wheeler Road.

Sunny knows every other dog that has run these woods as well. She sniffs like a vacuum cleaner over droppings and markings left by the parade of canines that travel these trails. We run into them often: Ted, Chloe, Ben, Casey. Sunny loves nothing as much as wrestling and leaping with her friends, fur cyclones nipping each other's ears, chasing each other through the underbrush and down the path. If there is mud or water, they will find it and not so much leap in as roll through every ounce.

We seek out her friends, even make play dates as if they were children in pre-school. Those who know understand that they are our children. We bring them together to get them used to others of their kind and make them sociable to our kind. At the heart of it, we bring them together because we believe it makes them happy.

But more often than not, it is just Sunny and me, out early when the morning mist has yet to burn off or when the temperatures sit near single digits. Sunny leaps from the backseat of the car with untethered eagerness, the singular definition of joy in the bounding run down the closest trail. This winter, the snow is deep and forms snug insulation throughout the woods, keeping it stinging cold and crystalline. From her very first forays off the leash in these woods, she has run ahead and then stopped....... turning to see if I am following. When she sees me lumbering behind, she gives me the impatient look of the child. "Are you coming???" Then she dashes off again.

When we are deep along the trails, marked by broken trees and long-forgotten rock walls, I am struck by the starkness of the whites and grays and browns of winter. Most people love the autumn woods with the dazzling splashes of reds and oranges and yellows. I do as well. But I love the winter woods the best. With these flattened tones, the canvas has no edges. It is monochrome and strangely sad except for the flash of golden tan and palomino white that is Sunny. She is all the color the woods need on these perfect mornings, as she pads along with a stick in her mouth on the winding trails.

We never set out to any destination. If we are ambitious, we walk along the river where the snow covers the water stones and rushes under the ice. We take the middle trail back up and toward the parking area, and I work up a good sweat under parka and wool. Sometimes we just wander in the direction of Spring Hill Road and Pope Road, but we never go that far. Sunny used to wander cautiously on the way out, sniffing carefully every inch of the trail, and then rush with unimpeded exuberance on the way back. She'd break into a mad puppy rush back and forth across the trails at full sprint, somehow avoiding poking branches and hidden stones.

Lately, she's calmed down and charges down the path rather than off into the underbrush. We worked ceaselessly on commands. "Sunny, come!!!" I would yell, and when she arrived, she'd get a treat and endless praise. Then a stranger might appear well down the path, and she instantly forgets everything we have worked on and charges off to greet him. Not everyone appreciates her enthusiasm. It remains a work in progress—social grace versus the very nature of her soul.

These walks were never intended to be anything more than required exercise for an energetic puppy. It was the woods themselves that transformed these morning forays. The woods are living entities that embrace the wanderers who come. There is nothing static in the trees and rocks and earth, it is a shifting landscape that moves with each new season and each new morning. Sunny has taken me into these woods and showed me the way in and around them. She has given me the gift of time spent quietly moving. Sometimes we don't know where we are going until we get there. Often, the getting there is not the point at all. ❑

# *Getting Ready For The Millennium*

My friend George's Aunt Florence is 102 years old. George has spent the last few years giving Aunt Florence goals to strive for, reasons to keep on living. He told her to keep going and hang on so that she can say she lived in three different centuries and two millennia. Lucid, with a rosy complexion, and still able to care for herself in her own apartment, Aunt Florence sighs and tells him she is just tired and is ready to die. She has seen more than a life-time's worth of wonder – wars and hurricanes, and the inexorable march of progress, from the advent of the telephone and the auto-mobile to watching a man walk on the moon. What more could she possibly want? How much living can one body do?

Nonetheless, tomorrow night, God willing, Aunt Florence along with the rest of us is going to step right into the start of the next thousand years. We will all have a kind of cataclysmic moment as the new day, the new year, the new century, and the new millen-nium sweep across the planet, time zone by time zone by time zone. You may be alone with the TV on, shivering out at First Night in Boston, blaring noisemakers at a gala black tie party, lying on a moonlit beach in Hawaii, standing in silence by the Wailing Wall in Jerusalem, or holding tight to your dearest love in front of the fireplace, in the calm of your own living room.

It is nothing more or less than the eve of possibility, a mark of time on the Western calendar that signals the end of something momentous and the beginning of something even more momentous. Aunt Florence can tell us what it feels like to not know the sound of airplanes in the sky or the blue-light flow of a television set. She can tell us that something is coming because it must; and to remain calm in the face of fear and uncertainty and doubt. It will never be as bad as we worry about or as good as we dream about. But it will most certainly be.

She can also tell us that there was a time when we all didn't take ourselves so seriously; when there was no giant, pulsing electronic media wave buzzing with the notion that something was going on and we'd better pay attention or we'd miss it. For the dawn of this new millennium is tainted with a frenzy, a fever that tends to negate the beauty of all the progress mankind has made over the past thousand years. For too many of the six billion inhabitants of this planet, life has become a bullet train that flies fast into every day, speeding toward short-term goals and prior arrangements, too often missing the station and missing the point.

One can rightly point out that it was those on the swiftest trains who changed the world over the past thousand years. Galileo and Shakespeare and Christopher Columbus; Michelangelo, Da Vinci, and Abraham Lincoln; Henry Ford, the Wright Brothers, and Jonas Salk; Einstein, Gandhi, Martin Luther King and Franklin Roosevelt were all immersed in the fluid speed of genius and determination. We owe them and tens of thousands of others like them for lifting us, collectively, up and up and up so that we arrive at this precipitous doorstep in an age of unprecedented prosperity and scientific enlightenment.

Yet in the midst of great optimism and hope, we also retain the nagging weight of despair. Not because of the continued presence of poverty, hunger, anger, bigotry, despotism and cruel ignorance – though surely these things cannot be dismissed. But more because it so often feels that the further forward we step, the further behind we go. So often it feels like the aphorism that we have not learned anything from history and are thus doomed to repeat it over and over.

Most likely, George will tell you, Aunt Florence has lived beyond the century mark because of an indomitable spirit, a remarkable will and an enviable calm. The baby boomers will attack the issue of mortality like no other generation in history as we push to live forever. There will be armies of Jack LaLannes showing off the remarkable resilience of the human body, as debilitating diseases and the deteriorating effects of old age are battled into submission. Soon there will be millions of people in the developed world living past the century mark in terrific health and prosperity.

What is still missing from the formula, however, is a similar focus on the spirit. The real battle of the new millennium will be a spiritual one, an educational one, a search for enlightenment. The Internet will be revealed as a giant vessel sending out lifelines and bringing together communities of people who grow increasingly frustrated with the sense of longing and emptiness that colors their lives. Living longer will be meaningless if we don't live better. If there ever was a kinder and gentler time, we need to find a way to carry its essence with us as we go forward. Maybe Aunt Florence can help us there.

If we are lucky, we will realize that we have built the foundation for a wondrous new age of seeing, knowing and embracing. So let's drink a cup of kindness, a long, slow swallow this time so that it lasts a thousand years. ❑

# Defining Life at the Hair Salon

I can't remember how long I've been going to Sal Tantillo in West Concord for my haircuts. It must be seven or eight years by now. Given my current follicular status, it's kind of amazing that Sal even knows my name. I ought to be in and out of his chair in five minutes. Truth to tell, there's just not that much there to cut.

But every month or so, even we bald guys need a trim to look sharp. Sal has cut my hair for my wedding, for public appearances, for my son's bar mitzvah, for a long list of important life moments. And over the years, my hair appointments have morphed into something more. My haircuts with Sal are really encounter sessions, discussions of life and philosophy and theology. I'm sure we've never talked about the weather or the stock market. We have strayed now and again and discussed Little League, corned beef, and bocce. Occasionally, Sal breaks into song with his sweet tenor voice that he has honed during years of barbershop quartet competitions.

What we've mostly had is a long, running conversation, a conversation between two middle-aged guys from very different backgrounds who have found common ground in a swivel chair in front of a mirror. And Sal, being the artiste he is, can transform a five-minute trim into a 40-minute extravaganza, just like that. When we get onto an intense subject, like religion or families, Sal seems to cut one hair at a time. He snips a bit here, a bit there.

He cleans up the back of my neck. He trims my beard. He does a shampoo.

Being Italian, born in Sicily and bred in the Bronx, Sal can stop in mid-trim, wave his scissors dramatically to make a point, and has yet to draw blood. Once, I'll admit, we really got going and he nearly shaved my head. It was short, let me tell you, and when I got home, my wife was not thrilled. I said, "Honey, we were talking about Jesus and one of the apostles. Sal was into it. What could I do?"

Sal loves to talk about the Bible, about Jesus, about the meaning of religion in his life. This Saturday, in fact, Sal is going to be ordained as a deacon at The Cathedral of St. Paul in Worcester. He will assist as deacon of the Mass the following day at his own church, St. Anna's in Leominster. It is a milestone moment for him, one that he has studied for for over a year. It is, in fact, a calling.

As a short, bald Jewish guy, I'm proud as hell of Sal. While I don't embrace his religious beliefs, I am more than impressed by his dedication and zeal. His is not the zeal of a missionary. He never proselytizes. He tells me stories from the Bible, stories that he has had to study and analyze and write homilies about. He listens when I tell him about Judaism; about my skepticism of organized religions, about how it seems that religion has actually served to pull men apart more than it has brought them together.

I've never really believed in God, at least not the God with a long white beard who watches over us in heaven and makes sure bad things won't happen. Not the God that people pray to in churches, synagogues and mosques. I do believe that the universe is a mysterious, unknown place and that there are forces at work well beyond our knowledge or understanding. I know, for example, that the love man summons into his life in the face of tragedy, despair, anger, hatred and fear must emanate from some special place. I've often wondered if I would find comfort in prayer, if I could ever bring myself to let go and stand in the shadows of my own uncertainty.

Sal has a gentle way of embracing Jesus and his faith. He has faced enough trauma in his own life to have come to the conclusion that this is as real as the air he breathes. When he tells me about some parable in the Bible, scissors raised high toward the fluorescent lights, I can feel that it is alive for him deep inside his soul. I may have too much cynicism to embrace the words, but I do envy the emotion.

And when he finally powders my neck and lifts the sheet from my shoulders, my cut hairs cascading to the floor, I check out his handiwork in the mirror, surprised that we are actually done. The conversation concludes for now, but I know, with Sal and me, we will pick up without missing a beat the next time, a lifetime's worth of joy and sorrow to discuss when the hair grows thick on the sides and the beard needs a trim. ❏

# What the Cardinal Sees

Every morning, just after dawn, the cardinal flies into the window.

From my bed, I hear him banging against the glass in the dining room or the bathroom. He does this repeatedly, sometimes for a half hour or more. When he first appeared, I was astounded. Why would a bird fling itself hard against a glass window over and over? I'd go and gaze from an upstairs window and watch this flash of bright red sit on a tree branch and then make a quick strike against the window and then fly back to the branch.

I asked some bird experts and they agreed that the cardinal believes it is chasing off an intruder. Being highly territorial, the cardinal sees a reflection of itself in the glass and flies at it, wings aflutter, to scare it away. In this case, the cardinal is literally its own worst enemy.

And lately I've begun to wonder whether this little red bird is nothing more than nature's clever representation of the human condition. We are, it is clear, our own worst enemy. We are a species that has been flinging itself against hard and dangerous surfaces for eons. Somehow, no matter how much damage we inflict upon ourselves, we limp back to our tree branch and find a way to fling ourselves yet again. There is no way to avoid the thought that we are, in the end, attacking our own reflection, over and over, to no avail.

Great philosophers have long wrestled with this remarkably consistent paradox of man's inhumanity to man. What would some of these philosophers, now long dead, think of the world we have fashioned today? This crowded, pulsing planet is straining with the tension of such a question. It is at the very core of human nature to find a way, to survive, to seek the light when covered with darkness.

But along the way, it sometimes feels so depressingly hard. To awake to orange-level terrorist alerts, to argue over the merits of a new war, to be constantly bombarded by images of violence, both real and imaginary ones created under the cloak of entertainment. We abhor violence yet we celebrate it in ways that past generations would find simply incomprehensible. We have finally succeeded in not only elevating but accepting violence as a legitimate form of art.

Tomorrow, I turn 50. A half-century. Born in the right place at the right time. Standing, still upright, maybe bent a bit from the strain. Such milestones that man embraces, looking for meaning and significance. I expect to celebrate this occasion because I have come, after a long and winding life, to understand how blessed I truly am. Born in the right place, at the right time, surrounded by people who flung themselves at windows to keep enemies and troubles and sadness away from my nest.

But I find my happiness and good fortune tempered by the state of this world that we cannot hide from or avoid, no matter how lucky we may be by birth and circumstance. I know that there are people of good will with kind and pure hearts who want desperately for an end to the madness. I know they are everywhere, and it is because of them that we have reason to reach for the light. They are the light.

Yet, we all feel this collective urge to scream out and put a giant healing hand on the heads and hearts of those who cannot find a way off their own tree branches, who cannot stop seeing their enemies in every glassy surface.

Listen to this poem, written by some anonymous person who summed it up so well.

This is the grave of Mike O'Day,
Who died maintaining his right of way.
His right was clear, his will was strong,
But he's just as dead as if he'd been wrong.

When you watch for half a century, you can't help feeling that the urge for humans to die maintaining their right of way is never going to end. There is this image of the cardinal, so beautiful and awe-inspiring, unable to distinguish what is real and what is reflection. It is perhaps the natural order of things, and part of our struggle is that we can never truly rise above it completely, even as we desperately wish we could.

For me, having been born on Valentine's Day, there is the small but real understanding that every day should celebrate love. Fifty years worth of birthdays has illustrated that there is something powerful in this embrace, powerful enough to counterbalance the pain and send cardinals away from disturbing reflections, off into the blue sky. ❏

# The Ride

In the fall of 1971, my parents and I loaded up our old station wagon with my clothes, a few books, a portable electric typewriter, and some great expectations and headed north to Boston. I was about to begin my freshman year at Boston University, a school that I'd chosen for many reasons, not the least of which were the 250 miles that separated it from my northern New Jersey home.

I have only a vague recollection of that drive through New York, Connecticut, and into Massachusetts. I remember that my heart began to beat faster as we headed east on the Massachusetts Turnpike and saw the first outline of downtown Boston looming ahead. I also remember the brutally hot day, carrying my things into the high-rise dormitory, and both my mother and sister crying as I gave them a farewell hug.

More than 31 years later, much has changed in all our lives. There have been deaths, births, several marriages, and a remarriage. I spent four wonderful years at BU and decided to stay in the Boston area, where I fashioned a life and a career. Like thousands of my fellow alumni from the metropolitan area, Boston and its environs lured us to set our roots, don Red Sox caps, and explain that Boston has most of the good things found in New York and far fewer of the bad.

And the thread across those three decades, the one thing that has never changed, is the drive between Boston and New Jersey, the 250 miles—give or take a few—that has defined my connection to my family all these years. I could not begin to count how many times I've made this journey: west along the Mass Pike, exit at Sturbridge, west on 84 through Hartford, Waterbury and Danbury, south on 684 through Westchester into White Plains, over the Tappan Zee Bridge, west on 287 to the Garden State Parkway South, and into the heart of New Jersey. And inevitably, back again in the reverse direction.

It is, in my unbiased opinion, the worst ride in the continental United States. If there is a more congested, dangerous and unpleasant set of roadways in this country, I've not heard of it. If there is a better testament to my love and devotion to my family than my willingness to repeat this nightmarish journey year upon year upon year just to be in their presence, I can't think what it could be. If I've said it once—that I'd never make that ride again—I've said it a thousand times. I know I mean it when I say it. But family ties are strong and insidious, and before long, there I am, back in a traffic jam outside Waterbury, Connecticut.

Keep in mind that my mother, two sisters, brother and their respective families all live in central New Jersey now, near Freehold and Princeton. They tend to think of Boston as just south of the Arctic Circle. They believe there is strength in numbers, and thus their logic is it is far easier for me, my wife and kids to go to them than it is for all fifteen of them to schlep to see us. Somehow,

I've bought into the theory, and so the road trip count, if it were possible to determine, is heavily weighted on my tires.

I've never truly analyzed what makes this ride so predictably awful. It almost always starts out benignly enough. Living west of Boston these days, we make our way west on bucolic Rt. 2 to Rt. 495 south and then west along Rt. 290 past Worcester. Easy enough. We get onto the Mass Turnpike only an exit from the Sturbridge toll plaza, and with our Fast Lane gadget stuck firmly to the windshield, we can now fly through the toll booths, laughing with glee at the poor saps waiting on long lines to pay cash. The dog is contentedly sleeping with her head on my son's lap in the backseat by now. "This isn't so bad," I always think to myself.

The trouble inevitably begins in Connecticut, a state without a major sports franchise or reason for being, other than to serve as a geographical barrier between Boston and New York. I'm convinced that Connecticut is an old Indian word meaning "Road Work Ahead." Over the course of 31 years, I've never traversed the length of Connecticut without stopping somewhere in L.A.-like traffic due to road repair. When anthropologists someday unearth the root cause of road rage, it will undoubtedly be found in Connecticut.

Though Hartford, when approached at the wrong time of day, can be a traffic nightmare, it is the aforementioned Waterbury that holds a special place in the Traffic Jam Hall of Fame. Is it the four lanes of highway converging into two lanes that causes the inevitable tie-up? Is there some special significance to the giant cross on the hill overlooking the highway that turns Waterbury into a religious experience? Is it simply Connecticut's way of saying "Take that, you snobby Bostonians, you rude New Yorkers!!??"

You might ask: Why not avoid Waterbury and take Rt. 91 south from Hartford onto 95 and through Stamford and Westchester? If you do ask, then you've obviously never driven on 95 from Connecticut into New York. I'm certain there is a full 30-minute stretch in any given 24-hour period when this part of 95 isn't a parking lot. I've just never been there to witness it.

Once out of Connecticut, my heart fills with hope. The respite offered by the 30-mile stretch of Rt. 684 through Katonah and Armonk lulls me into reverie, making me forget that the worst is still ahead. The big swing onto Rt. 287 jolts me back to reality. Suddenly and without warning, the volume of cars screaming toward the Tappan Zee is overwhelming. There is no mercy here. Don't bring beginners around here or they may return their permits. This is also a place where roadwork never ceases and five-mile backups to the bridge are almost inevitable.

By now, my blood pressure increases in inverse proportion to the speed of the bumper-to-bumper traffic. The slower we crawl, the more I need a scotch and water. Even the breathtaking sweep of the beautiful Tappan Zee Bridge as it spans the Hudson River near Nyack does nothing to soothe the pain. By now, I've been in the car for close to four hours. My back hurts. I have to pee. I regress to six years old. "Are we there yet?" my brain screams to my numb right knee.

When we finally make our way onto the Garden State Parkway and pass the Welcome to New Jersey sign, there is reason for optimism. First, there is the rest stop where both the dog and I can relieve our bladders. Then we pass through Paramus, my old hometown, which inevitably fills me with nostalgia for at least the two minutes it takes to pass the endless shopping malls that landscaped my youth.

Down near the Oranges, we find more Connecticut-like traffic. If we have the audacity to leave on a Friday afternoon, the Parkway is a slow torture of start and stop traffic, from toll plaza to toll plaza. Fumbling for exact change in the pre-EZ Pass days, every trip spawned the inevitable question: When did the Marquis de Sade have time to design this highway? Why did one unsightly New Jersey highway get encumbered by tolls every 30 feet when its ugly stepsister, the Turnpike, at least figured out that it makes more sense to pay when you get off?

And speaking of the New Jersey Turnpike, it is now the last part of our journey, the last test of courage and will. As we leave the Parkway at Exit 129, we fly onto the Turnpike toward Exit 8A Jamesburg/Cranbury, where my mother awaits with brisket and chocolate cake. However, there is no such thing as a free ride on this trip. As we reach Exit 9, the traffic stops dead without explanation. We are a tantalizing seven miles from our exit but it feels like a Wal-Mart parking lot on a Saturday morning before Christmas.

I've done this ride on holiday weekends and endured seven hours door to door. I've done the ride through the night when my father died, and I felt as if I were floating outside the car the entire way there. I've driven down for weddings, anniversaries, birthdays, bar mitzvahs and a lifetime's worth of family gatherings. I swear I'm never doing the ride again….until my mother comes out to the car, bursting with love and welcome, and says, "You made good time!" ❏

Spring

It was past the end of May, that much I remember, when the puppy bit me in a place so startlingly inconvenient that the scream was hurtling toward the ceiling before my ears could even hear it. We had come in from the new green grass in which she loved to roll and leap and sniff for hours. She also loved to munch on the grass, snatching mouthfuls out of the ground and chewing bits before I could sneak my finger past the sharp tiny teeth to remove what I could. It was after all that, back inside, when she was ostensibly calm, that she had one of those puppy moments, the electric jolts of pure energy that surge like lightning across a darkened sky. Playful, wiggling, nipping. My light cotton pajamas were not much of a defense and she got me, innocently, unintentionally, miraculously. The damage inflicted was minimal, but I had a sense that, with the change of seasons, this one would be outside......a lot. ❑

# Remain Calm and Share
# Your Bananas

I was in Provincetown the other night with my girlfriend, and we strolled past the town hall which was all aglow. Parked at the curb was a line of stretch limos, those long white ones with darkened windows that whisper to you that Madonna must be somewhere nearby.

But a glance up to the town hall told us otherwise. "Sure," we slapped our foreheads, it was Prom Night. A crowd of kids dressed in grownups' eveningwear surged out of the town hall. A simple spring Saturday night was transformed for them into one of those lifetime nights, a night to dress up and celebrate some unique rite of passage, to be part of a photograph that one day will produce shrieks of laughter from your kids.

Seeing these teenagers, dressed like adults and feeling some potent mixture of adolescent and adult feelings, standing on the doorstep to some unknown and unknowable future, made me think of my friend Annie.

Annie is Anne Lamott, a wonderful writer who lives in Marin County, north of San Francisco. She is best-known for two amazing books, "Operating Instructions" and "Bird by Bird." Those two books essentially present Annie's startlingly honest view of life and what it takes to be a single parent, to be a writer, be a sinner and a saint, and to weave a path through the raging jungle to humanbeinghood.

I read "Bird by Bird" last summer when I was in the midst of a co-dependent, shivering meltdown, a time when words of wisdom were desperately welcome. In that book was the hilarious and achingly painful truth about so many things we all struggle with, a truly honest account of how we are constantly finding ourselves trapped by our own idiosyncrasies in desperately dark corners, often chased there by unkind people we think we love but who, in reality, simply make us hold our breath. "You don't deserve to be treated without decency and respect," Annie admonished in her book. "You don't deserve to be made to hold your breath."

I found Annie on the Web and called her. I had to talk to someone with this kind of insight. We became email pen pals and she shared her thoughts and fears with me. She became my virtual street lamp when the darkness came.

Not long ago, she started writing a column on the Internet, a twice monthly offering called "Word by Word" on the Salon literary magazine site. Last spring, she penned a column called "B+ is Good Enough" which was in fact a speech she gave to a high school commencement in San Francisco.

She explained to these graduating seniors that it took her until age 35 to realize that B+ was good enough. She'd grown up as an overachieving perfectionist, a championship-level tennis player, honor roll student and budding writer whose parents served up the fuel for her fire. When she'd bring home a B+, her parents would shrug and say, "We're just wondering, if you did enough to get a B+, couldn't you have done that little bit more to get an A?"

For Annie, the drive that made her a best-selling author produced some unexpected side effects. She found that the book contracts and Jeep Cherokees just didn't produce the calm feeling of self-worth she'd expected. She could only feel good about herself after a few rounds of drinks. Her self-esteem got wrapped up in alcohol and drugs and bulimia and what she calls "black belt co-dependence" that nearly ruined her life.

Thank goodness she found her way, through AA and religion and remarkable friends and family, and her beautiful son Sam, back to the land of the living. She can now whine with the best of them, and her columns are both hysterical and poignant and touch so many chords they form a symphony.

And I was thinking, as I watched those kids in Provincetown, about how incredible it was that they were there, on that one special night, a few weeks before graduation, with so much at stake and so little awareness of what lay ahead.

I wanted to climb onto one of those limos and start yelling, "B+ is good enough!" I wanted to mail each of them the column by Annie so that they'd know there is at least one honest adult out there who is willing to tell them the truth. I remembered how I had left high school with unbelievable expectations, my own and those of my parents, my friends and classmates, and then spent two more decades reeling from the effort of trying to cross an uncrossable chasm.

Now that I'm a parent myself, I understand fully the intoxication of that love, how we want our kids to be the best soccer player and pianist and artist, to get the scholarships and the best jobs and the best houses. I understand how we want them to achieve to their full potential and suck in only the richest juices that life can offer.

But as we approach graduation day, how many of those beautiful young men and women have been handed the wrong operating instructions? How many understand that B+ is really good enough and that the tally at the end of that long road is about trying your best and expecting failures as well as successes. That at the end of the day, the self-worth comes from the self, not the worth.

Perhaps I'd give them another message from Annie. In a recent column, she describes coming upon a "Mantra for the American Jungle" on a trip to San Diego. She liked it so much she wrote it on her hand so she wouldn't forget. And come graduation day, maybe we should tell the senior class this: "Remain calm, and share your bananas." ❏

# The Sea of Tranquility

When I was a teenager and the space capsules were floating around the moon, I remember watching those grainy television images of the lunar surface as the historic landing grew, mission by mission, closer to reality.

In particular, I remember being struck by the name of one landing site, the Sea of Tranquility. Juxtaposed against the forbidding black, white and gray lunar landscape, the Sea of Tranquility was a name that touched some chord deep within me, the lyrical sound of a place of infinite calm and quiet beauty. "Houston," the crackly, static-filled message finally came from the astronauts, "Tranquility Base here…..the Eagle has landed."

My search, over a lifetime, for my own Sea of Tranquility continues. My capsule hurdles across landscapes, wondrous and immense, and yet I often feel as if the eagle has never landed and never will.

More often than is wise or healthy, I feel wellsprings of anger that control my life and push my ship further and further from Tranquility base. I feel such pulsing anger in the world around me as well, see it in the faces of fellow drivers who take it personally, as I too often do, if the person in front of me is driving too slowly. I sense it in the stores and restaurants and workplaces, where anger has become a ubiquitous presence, lurking close to every surface, ready to explode from the tiniest of sparks.

I know anger too well. Maybe you do too. While love may be the most powerful emotion, anger is the most debilitating, the most destructive, the most capable of eating into your soul and visiting you in the darkest part of the night. A long feud with an ex-spouse or co-worker or boss simmers like a pot over an eternal flame. Anger is cumulative and feeds on itself, growing like the alien spore in "Little Shop of Horrors" into a giant hungry plant that demands, "Feed Me!" More and more, medical evidence suggests that stress and anger have a direct correlation to heart disease and other health problems.

We live in an age superbly suited to anger. The world spins round in a frenzy of stimuli and mounting noise. Technology and the wired society have kicked that noise up a notch; more to know, more to learn, information overload, race out in front or get left behind. The number of gadgets we've come to depend on—from computers to cell phones—mounts. The more complex the device, the more likely it is to break or remain incomprehensible. Mounting as well is the time we waste on unhelpful help lines, cursing at recorded voices that tell us to hang on. We are hanging on…..barely.

Demands on every front crush inward—children, jobs, relationships, debt, health, fitness—with an unceasing sense that the faster you go, the further you get behind. Anger flows easily into this scenario. Frustration built upon doubt manifested by a general sense that time is the only real and valuable commodity, and there is never enough of it. Anger springs from each of us for individual reasons, from crises hidden in the deep recesses of the past, from character flaws or psychological episodes we may not remember and may never understand.

And all this pre-Millennium angst has spawned an entire industry devoted to spirituality and healing and self-discovery. The best-seller list is crowded with self-help guides to serenity and spirituality and ways to control the feelings of powerlessness and anger. But "self-help" may, in fact, be the oxymoronic buzzword of our time. Helping yourself is what you do best in the buffet line, not necessarily on the road to emotional well-being.

And getting help is not simple either. The serious and honest practitioners are crowded in with the charlatans, and the path to true tranquility seems like an axiom for the lost in Maine: "you just can't get theyah from heyah." We buy and read, listen to talk radio, and watch seminars on PBS, trek to our shrinks and yet the world's collective anger continues to generate atomic heat.

Anger itself has become a form of sport and entertainment. No one raises an eyebrow when Jerry Springer, with his patented anger television, passes Oprah in the ratings. The World Wrestling Federation turns a public's fascination with anger and in-your-face screaming fury—real or phony—into huge profits. In a world of disaffection, anger becomes the currency and the common ground.

We are, of course, not trapped in all this anger unless we allow ourselves to be. There are choices to be made and attention to be paid. The answer may lie for you in a book by Chopra or a poem by Walt Whitman. The answer may lie on a therapist's couch or a long run in the early morning mist. The answer may lie in the look on the face of your three-year old while you throw a tantrum in the next traffic jam. The answer may be as simple as memorizing Niebuhr's Serenity Prayer, the one about accepting with serenity the things that cannot be changed, courage to change the things that should be changed, and the wisdom to distinguish one from the other.

You never know where and when the epiphany will come. But if you are like me, you want to believe that your sea of tranquility lies somewhere closer than the moon. ❏

# A Search for Meaning in Another Life

Not long ago, a friend gave me a wonderful present: a gift certificate for a genuine Thai massage with Joseph Kappel, a gentle giant of a man, who works at Yoga for Life and the Healing Essence in West Concord.

Thai massage is unlike any that you might get at your local health club. Using his massive hands and feet, Kappel kneads and prods your muscles deeply, to the edge of pain and sometimes beyond. The massage is done in combination with deep breathing and a sort of meditative concentration, all designed to call up the stress and tension of our lives and expel it through Kappel's touch.

As he worked on me, Joseph Kappel told me a story that was enthralling, far beyond the massage itself. Kappel, it turns out, spent 20 years as a Buddhist monk in monasteries in Thailand and England. In saffron robes, with shaved head and a searching heart, Kappel meditated, prayed, and studied scripture alongside a family of devout believers in the quiet, reflective Buddhist life. He lived the austere existence of the deeply devoted: celibate, one meal a day, hours of meditation and prayer, long treks through the forests of northeast Thailand and later the countryside of northern England, all in the search for enlightenment in a religious philosophy foreign and befuddling to most Americans.

It was a leap, perhaps as far a leap as one can make, for the former high school athletic star from Seattle; a middle-class kid whose father was a barber and mother a clerk at JC Penney. It was even more of a leap for Kappel, who had just finished a year-long tour of duty in Vietnam where he flew reconnaissance helicopters and won a Silver Star for valor in combat.

Kappel's transformation to Buddhist novitiate was not the trendy 60s campus radical variety. He'd quit junior college after a single semester and enlisted in the army as an MP. He quickly qualified for officer's candidate school and left as a first lieutenant. From there, he enrolled in flight school, emerged as a captain and combat helicopter pilot, and shipped off to Southeast Asia.

Kappel's unit was the First Cavalry, depicted graphically in the film "Apocalypse Now." Like their military predecessors, these cavalry soldiers were at the front of the action, scouts and warriors who simply traded horses for helicopters. Kappel flew in hunter-killer tandem teams, his Light Observation Helicopter skimming above the treetops searching for the enemy while the massive Cobra choppers flew above and rained terror down when an enemy was sighted. Kappel flew 600 hours and countless missions, getting shot down once and dodging 50-caliber anti-aircraft bullets numerous times. He was never wounded physically, but he knew that he had killed at least one man and probably many more in fulfilling his duty.

And like most who served in this strange and terrible war, Kappel was deeply conflicted about the killing, even as he tore through the sky above the dense jungles of Vietnam. As a child, Kappel had felt a longing to understand the meaning of his life, and Vietnam only served to re-awaken this longing. A year in this Conradian heart of darkness brought only more questions and feelings of disconnection.

While in Vietnam and on R&R trips to neighboring Thailand, Kappel encountered Buddha for the first time. He felt drawn to this image, putting a picture of Buddha in his tent and later wearing the Buddha's image around his neck instead of a cross.

On trips to Thailand, he sought books and information on Buddhism and began to read and learn. The conflict within him grew stronger, even as he continued to fulfill his duty, compiling an impeccable record and winning the Silver Star.

When Kappel returned to the U.S. in 1970, he felt the pull more than ever and realized what path was set for him. He first had to get a discharge from the military which still owned another 18 months of his life. After applying for a conscientious objector discharge and undergoing rigorous scrutiny about his sincerity, Kappel was granted CO status, left the army, and returned to Thailand. He joined the Wat Bovorn monastery in Bangkok and later went to study in the remote forest of northeast Thailand under a renowned Buddhist monk named Ajahn Chah.

At first, his family and friends believed he had lost his mind. "I don't know if anybody really knew what I was doing," Kappel recalls. For Kappel, the commitment was consuming and complete. He embraced the teachings of Buddha with the fervor of the converted, and he never looked back.

The meditation, the self-reflection, the gentle calmness of the monastic life suited him for a long time. When Ajahn Chah grew gravely ill, Kappel tended to him and learned the art of Thai massage from a master who had been called to his teacher's bedside. He left the Thailand forest in 1984 and moved to a monastery outside Newcastle in northern England for seven more years. There he was the subject of a BBC documentary and gained renown even in the U.S. for his work.

I asked Kappel to sum up these 20 years, and he smiled. "It was a wonderful education and foundation for living life in a really full and awake state," he says. "It was a journey, and the journey continues."

In 1991, Kappel began to feel that he needed to continue his education elsewhere, and he removed his robes, put on civilian garb for the first time in two decades, and re-entered a strange and unfamiliar life. "The things I had to learn and grow from couldn't have happened in the monastery," he says simply. He returned to the U.S. and faced not only deep culture shock but a poignant question: what does an ex-monk do, and where does he go?

Kappel ended up in Massachusetts, studying stress therapy at the UMass Medical Center in Worcester. His new friends lived in Cambridge and Watertown and Boston, but after a few years in the urban environment, teaching stress reduction in Massachusetts prisons, the longing returned for the quiet of the forest. The green of Concord was a powerful lure, and he rented a room and began to look for customers.

At 6'2", 240 pounds, with a shock of curly dark hair, Kappel, now 49, remains a stranger in a strange land. He says he misses the connection to the community that the monastery provided. But he is excited about the potential "of what is possible in my own life now." He remains a Buddhist, meditates daily, and teaches meditation and stress reduction for a living rather than as a calling. He is training for a commercial pilot's license and hopes to fly helicopters again, albeit in a more peaceful setting. In many ways, Kappel is trying to recapture his past and construct a life in which he can be as awake as possible, awake to reaching the fullest that life is capable of providing.

If you get a chance, drop in and get a massage. You'll be awakened, take my word for it.  ❏

# Lessons Learned At Little League

I am standing near the bench at a town Little League field while my ten-year old son stands at the ready in the batter's box. Here is what he sees: the bases are filled with his teammates, the score is tied, there are two outs, the pitcher holds a small white sphere that he is about to fire in his direction and, if things go awry, might smack him in the head and hurt a real lot.

I am the assistant coach, unwilling to be the manager because my temperament is ill-suited to the tidal waves of pain and joy and sorrow that ten-year old boys must endure to compete in Little League. In my role, I need never lose my patience or make tough decisions about why Tyler is in right field rather than at shortstop. Here, the buck slips past and never stops by me, which is just fine and right and proper.

Mostly I am here because I believe that my presence will help my ten-year old play the game better. I believe this because this theory worked extremely well when he was six, seven, eight, even nine, and Little League was a different animal.

Now, at this level, things have gotten serious. The kids pitch to each other (at lower levels, we coaches would toss cream puffs to our own players so they could smack them and get hits and feel awesomely talented). At this level, an umpire calls balls and very liberal strikes and there is no forgiveness or seven or eight more chances. This is where the wheat starts to get separated from the chaff, and there is no hiding the fact that some of the boys can catch and throw and hit and make the plays, and some of the boys can't.

There are umpires and standings and playoffs and the first real whiffs of that unmistakable scent called pressure. It is still fun, but fun has become a tiny byproduct. What it is is a taste of real life disguised as a recreational youth activity. And because of this, it is good and visceral and unremittingly tortuous for the species that set all this up: the parents.

And so I am at this field, my boy is at the plate, and all I want is for something good to emerge from this moment. My boy is not the big, aggressive, agile and athletic one. He is the timid, sweet one with the smile of an angel, the heart the size of Jupiter, and the athletic genetics of his mother whose closest brush with sports was tossing my basketball shoes in the closet back when we were married. But he plays baseball because I immersed him in the beauty and poetry of the game from the moment I could get his little hand to hold a baseball.

He plays because we have spent more hours than I can count in the backyard or the park, catching and throwing and hitting and pretending he was the shortstop for the Red Sox and made all the greatest plays in history. He plays because I always believed that there was something good about being part of a team and learning how it felt to win and lose and participate. And mostly he plays because he really wants to.

He has refused soccer and football and basketball. But baseball has been his, a glove tied up with a baseball and soaked with neat's-foot oil under his bed as a talisman of the season to come.

And perhaps I shouldn't be here anymore because the tension inside me billows to absurd proportions when my son is in the spotlight of the game. The season has gotten off to a horrible start, and our team has yet to win, and my son has yet to actually hit the ball. We have reached a juncture where a groundball of any kind would be victory, where I ache for him to avoid yet another failure. I am well-grounded in the team mentality and know logically that I shouldn't be fixated on his performance. This is a bunch of ten-year olds, for crying out loud. Get a grip, I think to myself.

I wish I could report that the pitcher fired in a smooth one and that my son launched a base hit into left field, driving in two runs. But he stood in, brave as a soldier, and didn't flinch or move his bat as the ball floated tantalizingly and agonizingly straight over the plate.

"Strike three!" the umpire yelled.

And there in that moment when he turned back to the bench, his face red, and searched out my eyes, I felt the very rope of the journey that ties him to me, as it tied me to my father, and he to his. I felt the rip of having to hand him this imperfect world, where failure is a rite of passage and so much depends on chances taken on sunny Saturday afternoon diamonds. And I managed, because I am the grownup after all, to swallow that giant ache and hand him his glove and send him into right field with a sturdy "we'll get 'em next time, big guy."

Inevitably, he did get that first hit, and we won our first game, and there was the soaring joy of triumph that makes us want to play these games. But I believe I learned more about us during the struggle. There is, I have come to understand, real joy in Mudville, even after the strikeouts and errors and the games have ended. The joy is in the steely bond that brings fathers out with sons to don their gloves and toss the ball across green fields of love and devotion. The joy is in the being there, together, win or lose, etched forever in a churning life.  ❏

# Losing Aunt Elaine

Here is something my mother taught me: you can have a friend so dear, so loving, so entrenched in your life that you teach your children to call that person aunt or uncle, as if they were related by blood.

And there they are, in your life, so deep and far into the past that they precede your memories of childhood. They were simply always there.

Being lucky enough to have people like this in my life is one of the blessings, one of the many blessings, my mother gave me. Teaching your children the deep meaning of friendship is one of the indelible lessons, so taken for granted, that a person can pass along.

My mother's friend Elaine died of cancer the other day. Her funeral was on what would have been her 78th birthday. I hadn't seen Aunt Elaine all that often over the adult years of my life. Yet she had always been there in my childhood, with her husband, Uncle Jerry, and her own children. Uncle Jerry was a sweet man, a good friend to my father, and when he died of cancer, on the eve of my bar mitzvah, I cried and tried to understand this unfamiliar idea that a grownup could suddenly be gone, leaving a family, leaving friends, leaving me, to fill in an empty space amid the sorrow.

Aunt Elaine soldiered on alone. She had a successful career as a retail executive, raised three wonderful, loving children, and remained to the very end a dear and loving friend to my mother. She was there when my father died, also far too young, and left my mother bewildered and unprepared for her life ahead. I don't know what their conversations were, but my mother spoke to her often on the telephone, sharing the most meaningful pieces of her life, mostly her children's lives.

Their friendship lasted, remarkably, 61 years. Think of it, 61 years! Coping with the sadness and grief, my mother understands what an incredible gift this was, a gift of such surpassing value that you cannot measure it beyond the scope of itself. Aunt Elaine's passing is profound for so many reasons for my mother, not the least of which is the sense of wonder and despair that we face when our lives wind toward their conclusions and our lifetime friends begin to die.

In the past few weeks, two of my closest friends were diagnosed with cancer. I took this as a tragic coincidence but in reality, at age 50, I too am entering a new phase of life where vulnerabilities start to appear in places I always assumed were safe. I have no idea how to cope with these types of events. As for most people, the C-word has always been a nasty nightmare for me, a cataclysmic surprise that lurks and waits and pounces when we least expect it. My two friends were just minding their own business, living their lives, handling their aggravations and their pleasures, and suddenly everything changed. By some divine grace, they will both recover. Yet I cannot help but think that they will never feel completely safe again.

Confronting the scourges of our lives, whatever form they may take, requires a courage and will that seems impossible to access. Given devastating news, I expect to be devastated. Yet every passing moment makes me wonder why that part of life is so incredibly difficult. Illness, sorrow, confusion, and death are inevitably interwoven in the quilt of life. We put out our hands, palms outward, to ward it off, but there it is, ticking like an old clock, moving like a field of grain in a strong wind.

And so close to me, a guide and a muse, is my mother, who lost her sweet friend but refused to lock the doors and shutter the windows.

She grieves for her friend but, in her place, my mother will fill back up with her incalculable optimism and joy. She will be the center of the love of a family that worships her for her remarkable embrace of life and spirit. She will hold her many other wonderful friends a bit more tightly and understand how the gifts of this life are only lent, not given, for however long we have them. She will share the universal truth that raises us above this troubling world and makes us so human: the ability to love and be loved in the shadow of sorrow and the light of joy. ❏

# The Game at 50

I've stolen the ball at the top of the key. I turn and charge upcourt, dribbling frantically toward my basket. Out front to my left is George, the writer, racing out to lead the fast break. On the right is Herb, the minister, ready to fill the lane. Directly in front of me is Juice, the telephone guy, a menacing 6'5" defender awaiting my decision. Pass to George? Maybe Herb? Instead, I go right at Juice, leap with a grunt, soar skyward over his head, and slam dunk the ball with two hands through the hoop.

That scenario really happened, no kidding. Well, all except the last part. My soaring days are over. In truth, they never really began. As a short, gravity-bound 50-year old, basketball for me is played close to the ground. Dunking is what I do with an Oreo in milk. I actually tried to pass the ball to Herb, but Juice stuck out his big mitt, stole it, and tossed it back to his team at the other end. The guy who was supposed to be guarding me put in a lay-up.

Basketball is nothing if not dreaming. Guys like me play not just because we love the game, but because we need the game. Barring a blizzard, a poorly-timed appointment, or dire illness, I am here in this little bandbox of a gym in Concord, Mass. at noon on Mondays, Wednesdays and Fridays, from September through May. For an hour, a ragtag group of players ranging in age from mid-20s to over 50 race up and down the court, fire at will, attempt terrible passes, argue endlessly over ticky-tack fouls, sweat a lot, and leave the real world outside.

The wonderful thing about basketball is that even though I don't endorse a line of designer sneakers and my vertical leap is the height of a credit card, I can still have Michael Jordan moments. I can still fake my defender to the right, drive to the hoop and drop in a nifty lay-up—not very often, I grant you—but often enough to draw the grudging grunts of appreciation from my teammates and enough to keep me showing up for more.

For guys like me, basketball is the last real link to adolescence, to the stubborn notion that we can defy time and not look ridiculous in tank tops and baggy shorts. Last year, I turned 50 in February, three days before Michael Jordan turned 40. The media was abuzz about Jordan. He was still an All-Star, an icon, a one-man industry, rich as Croesus, and svelte in his NBA togs. Not even my lunchtime gang noticed my birthday. Turning 50 is no big deal anymore. George is already 54, and he pretty much outruns everyone in the gym. Tom, the CEO, is 51, and he hasn't missed a jump shot since the senior Bush was in the White House.

But it is a milestone for me. If someone had told me at age 13, when I started playing basketball, that I'd still be out there three days a week at age 50, I would have gagged on my chocolate milk. Fifty was old...too old for a game that requires speed, agility, quickness, and jumping ability.

Of course, turning 50, I haven't employed quickness or agility in more than a decade. I now rely on experience and guile. It isn't pretty. But we play in empty gyms so nobody's watching anyway. Every once in a while, the ragged game turns sweet and smooth. Every few weeks, I find my elusive jump shot and make basket after basket with the inexplicable rhythm they call "the zone." Mostly, I chase the guy I'm defending, hacking at his arms, grabbing at his jersey to prevent an embarrassingly easy lay-up. One thing that hasn't changed is the intense desire to win. In a world filled with ambiguity, basketball is pure black and white. You win or you lose. Slackers who don't care are not welcome in these games.

Twenty years ago, an orthopedist told me I was just a knee injury waiting to happen. "Give up basketball," he instructed. "Take up golf. It's safer." I didn't give his orders a moment's heed. Those who play know it is not a habit easily kicked. Michael Jordan has a decade on me, but after last season he finally retired for good. I chuckle at that. Retire? Nonsense. I'm shooting for 60. ❏

# I Am Waiting for Commencement

*In 1956, Lawrence Ferlinghetti wrote a moving and lyrical poem entitled "I Am Waiting." No one can reconstruct the beauty and power of his work, and I wouldn't even try. But I am borrowing liberally anyway, and I wanted the plagiarism police to know that I know, and it's too bad. Go read his poem, and you'll see what I mean. It is graduation time, so here is mine:*

I am waiting for my ship to come in.
And I am waiting for the perfect moment when high school dissolves into gilded memory.
I am waiting for the perfect tan.
And I am waiting perpetually for my parents to leave the room, quietly.

I am waiting for a sunrise over the Atlantic ocean that moves me to tears.
And I am waiting for a lover who puts the cap back on the toothpaste while she touches my soul.
I am waiting for my car at the body shop.
And I am waiting for someone to tell someone to tell anyone to stop the killing and the hatred and the despair.
And I am waiting, perpetually, for the world to be mine.

I am waiting for my sister to get out of the bathroom.
I am waiting for a night ride under a harvest moon.
And I am waiting for a time when grades and attendance and rules will be absent from my life.
And I am waiting, seemingly forever, for my skin to clear.

I am waiting for the television to be turned off.
I am waiting for speech patterns that don't revolve around the word like.
I am waiting for an honest, guileless, wordless look of understanding from someone over 30.
I am waiting desperately, passionately, for my heart to stop breaking.
And I am waiting endlessly for a summer that will not end.

I am waiting for the weekend when I pack up the car and drive away from this town.
I am waiting for tears to fall when my friends say goodbye.
I am waiting for my cynicism to be reborn as wonder.
And I am waiting for my time to be up and my number to be called.

I am waiting for the sky to fill with cumulus clouds and satin birds.
I am waiting for another chance.
And I am waiting for the loneliest night to end and the dawn that will follow.

And I am waiting for that one person who will change my life forever.

I am waiting for a flight to a setting sun.

I am waiting for passion and lust and raw unbridled emotion.

I am waiting for my life to finally begin.

"And I am awaiting, perpetually and forever, a renaissance of wonder." ❏

Summer

Janie and I liked to run along Rt. 62, down Harrington, and over to the old abandoned rifle range that snaked for a few miles through the woods. We weren't fast, but we kept a steady pace, and the path through the woods offered up enough rocks and snarled roots to trip up younger, more agile runners than us. I always ran behind, along the rutted way, single file because the path was not wide enough for side by side. I liked to watch her run; she was the only woman I'd ever dated who enjoyed exercise as much as I did. We were getting ready for the five-mile July 4th fun run that Concord sponsors every year, and that first year we would cross the finish line, hand in hand, arms raised in victory though we were near the back of the pack. "This is a woman I could marry," I thought to myself in the heat of the morning sun. ❑

# *Most Of The Will Is The Motion*

This is a summer of passionate heat, aggressive, blanketing heat that builds by the day and etches a memorable persona. What will you remember of the summer of '97? Dying lawns, steamy sleepless nights, the revitalizing surge of a dive through an ocean wave?

For me, this has been a summer of constant motion. In mid-September I will embark for the second year in a row on a 300-mile bicycle journey from Boston to New York City. I will be in the company of nearly 3000 committed souls who have signed up for the Boston-New York AIDS ride, a whirling crusade, a movable feast, a lifetime journey that lasts three days.

I wrote a story for this paper about my first AIDS ride last fall. Having completed this daunting challenge just weeks before, the euphoria and the incredible sense of accomplishment were still very much alive within me. Anything is possible, I wrote.

Anything. Like the patently absurd idea of actually doing this again.

Whatever happened to "been there, done that."

Let me be clear about one thing: this is not addictive. This I could live without. This is work. This is about grinding out mile after mile in the blast furnace heat of tarmac and hills. This is about lacing up running shoes at the crack of dawn to pound out three or four miles through the old rifle range near Harrington Street before the workday begins. This is joining 30 other riders on an early morning 48-mile training ride out to the hills of Harvard and pushing until your thighs are screaming and other parts of your anatomy have simply gone numb.

Let's face it, if man was meant to ride a bike to New York, God wouldn't have created the Delta Shuttle. The training, you have to understand, is really a day at the beach compared to the ride itself. Last year, I was a neophyte, nervous with anticipation and dread that I was taking on way too much; that I'd never be able to ride that far over hills that had taken on mythic proportions when discussed by those who'd done the ride before. By the time we were ready to leave the World Trade Center near Boston Harbor, I had visions of Everest, suddenly plopped in the middle of Connecticut, surrounded by foothills named K2 and Kilimanjaro.

Last year, the ride covered more than 300 miles and was spaced over four days. The middle two days held the "killer hills" in the Connecticut River Valley. And believe me, Everest has nothing on some of these babies. They ascend, like Gulliver's staircase, up and up and up again. And better men and women than me, younger, buffed out, muscles in places I don't have places, were walking those hills.

So this year, the fear of the unknown has simply been replaced by the fear of the known. The difference is that I did it! I made it to the finish at the Chelsea Piers in lower Manhattan, riding through the Bronx, past the Grand Concourse where my grand-mother lived when she was alive, down Fifth Avenue through the bumper cars, buses and oblivious cab drivers. I rode in amid the cheers and tears of my fellow riders who had become my imme-diate family for those four incredible days. It was something, let me tell you.

And so I signed up again, one more time around the dance floor. Last year, I was seeking a challenge. This year, calmer, happier, more focused, I let myself be coerced by my buddy John, an ortho-pedic surgeon from Beverly, who wanted to feel the experience for himself. I also had a deep suspicion that long about late August, I'd be kicking myself for missing the opportunity, because this is a challenge that is personal and universal at the same time.

I spend most of my year worrying about paying the bills, raising my son, meeting deadlines, staying healthy, picking a movie on a Friday night. I leave my conscience in my checkbook drawer, sending annual donations to charity, doing just enough to assure myself that a life of goodness is its own reward.

But this ride turns that on its ear. This ride translates into real dollars for AIDS clinics in Boston and New York City, into payment for lab tests and treatments and protease inhibitors that affect lives of real people hammered by this nasty bitch of a disease. This ride means that, for three days in September, I'm out on some blazing hot or rain-soaked Connecticut back country road, pedals whirling, back aching, eyes squinting against the wind and sun and grit, seeking some tiny piece of redemption.

And finding it.....in the faces of the other riders and the inexplicable comfort of another chance taken. Finding it in the incredibly compelling realization that you can, in fact, lose yourself in an act of doing good; selfishness through selflessness, mile after endless mile. As songwriter Chris Smither wrote, "Most of the will is the motion; most of the rest is devotion." ❏

# Sore Butts And Hearts Of Angels

Somewhere just north of New Haven, I started to question my usually rational mind. Here I am, I thought, pedaling and pushing and toughing out yet another mile, and another and another, over a patch of unfamiliar real estate. My neck and shoulders are on fire, my butt is sore, my legs are starting to get that rubbery feel, the way Sonny Liston's must have felt shortly before a Cassius Clay left hook sent him to the Lewiston canvas once upon a time.

For some reason, I kept thinking of a line from my last column. If God had intended for man to ride a bicycle to New York, he wouldn't have created the Delta Shuttle. And let me be real clear, that line stopped being funny long about the Connecticut border.

This, as you might have guessed by now, was the Boston-New York AIDS ride, a 260-mile bicycle jaunt from downtown Boston to lower Manhattan. My apologies if I'm sounding like a one-trick pony. I can only promise that this will be my very last column on this subject.....at least until next year.

The ride, which took place in mid-September on what turned out to be a glorious, rain- and hurricane-free weekend, was my second go-round for this amazing journey. Last year, after a bout with Hurricane Fran, the ride left me spent but exhilarated, amazed at what I had just done. This year, the feelings were similar in some ways but quite different overall. There's nothing like that first time, in love, in politics, in long-distance bike rides.

For me, the ride was like seeing a great movie the second time. This year, I got to notice all the details, the tiny moments of both pain and excitement that might have passed unnoticed a year ago. In my heart, I knew I could make the ride, go the distance. So that worry was replaced by the very cognitive notion of staying healthy, not falling, not getting hit by a car, and not boring my fellow riders to death with stories of last year's ride.

I wondered if this massive group of 3,200 people, an incredibly disparate group of beings, old and young, men and women, black and white and brown and yellow, gay and straight, would coalesce into a rolling family the way we did last year. I gauged my feelings, both physical and emotional, as the days evolved, from that early morning adrenaline rush to that evening fatigue when the body is working on sheer will and nothing more.

What was more clear this year than last was that the ride was a series of moments, of chance encounters with strangers who became brothers and sisters with hearts of angels in spandex shorts. I stopped at one of the interminable red lights that plagued us from southwestern Connecticut until the very tip of Manhattan. My neck and shoulders hurt so deeply from arching over the handlebars in a way that God definitely did not intend. I tried to rub my neck when I felt a pair of hands take my shoulders and start massaging. I looked over and there was an angel named Alison who smiled and said "Maybe this will help a little." And she gave me the best 30-second massage I'll ever have. When the light changed and with the ebbs and flows of the ride, I never saw her again, not even at the finish.

I rode every mile except one. I walked the last major hill at the end of our 97-mile ride on the first day. I wish I had that hill back, to be honest, but I had nothing left to give and two more days to ride, so discretion turned out to be the better part of valor. I felt fortunate that this year I had chosen to ride with my friend John, a superior athlete who arrived at camp an hour before me and had the tent set up and waiting each night. I wondered if I was among the turtles, until we got on the dinner line and met a road crew member who told us there were a thousand riders still out on the road, in the dark, struggling home.

We did become a family, just like last year. I believed that these riders were heroes, even before we left Boston. This was confirmed along the way, when someone fell from their bike and a dozen hands reached out to help them up. And it was further confirmed when we rode down 8th Avenue in New York City in front of tens of thousands of cheering people who gave us our Lindbergh moment, a moment that none of us will ever forget. People laughed, and wept, and drank in the river of emotion.

The closing ceremony was marked by a quiet that fell over the huge crowd. The ride director spoke of why we were there, why we had done this Herculean task. He spoke about those who were not there and had died from AIDS, and about how we had come to honor them with this ride. Down the center of 8th Ave, two people pulled an empty bicycle, slowly moving it through the riders toward the stage. With this ride, he said, we bring them back to us and tell them that we have not forgotten and that there is still a fight to fight,and the battle is not yet won.

Indeed. We raised $7.5 million on this ride, and it will give real aid to people at centers in Boston and New York and beyond. But the rides will have to continue because the battle is not yet won, not even close.

And yet the best thing that came from the ride, this second time around, was the very wonderful illustration that small communities of people can come together to really make a difference, as Margaret Mead once said. In fact, it is the only way that it happens. ❏

# Dog Days of Summer

It is a steamy Friday evening in June. Most civilized people are sitting down to barbecued hamburgers and a much-deserved beer or heading to their cozy summer rentals on the Cape and the Vineyard.

Not me.

I am sitting in the basement of the Harvey Wheeler Center in West Concord. I am surrounded by a legion of haggard, beleaguered people who bear the look of expectation usually found on the faces of pilgrims on the way to Lourdes. There is quiet desperation in their eyes—in my eyes—and we believe that we have come to a place of salvation and redemption. This, for the uninitiated, is Puppy Kindergarten.

Next to us, panting in a strange syncopated rhythm, are a pack of puppies, every size and breed you can imagine, from Airedales to Golden Retrievers. They are panting because they've just finished a 30-minute romp around the basement; a mad incomprehensible scrum of canines racing after each other, tackling, nipping, barking, leaping and licking each other in a brilliant planned effort to get their collective ya-yas out. Puppies love nothing so much as wrestling around with other puppies, regardless of the breed or size, and this is as close to puppy nirvana as it gets. Owners love it as well because it wears out the adorable critters and takes some of the Jolt Cola out of their little puppy veins.

But then the bell rings. Nervous owners move to leash their respective baby animals and settle down next to them on the floor in a giant oval circle. Class is about to begin. It may be called kindergarten but it feels more like basic training. In the center of the room stands our drill sergeant, Arlee Recktenwald, who has been running puppy training classes at Harvey Wheeler for the past 20 years. Arlee barks out orders to the owners and repeats herself two or three times on each point because owners can be incredibly dumb. Arlee subscribes to the theory that there are no bad dogs, just bad owners. What she tells us from the beginning, and over and over again, is that these adorable little babies are ANIMALS, not people.

If we treat them like people rather than descendants of wolves, which is what they are, we will be hopelessly lost in bringing obedience into their peculiar little lives. If we babble baby talk to them and let them "just be puppies," we will end up with intolerable creatures rather than loving pets. Animal shelters are filled with dogs who were hopelessly lost to good but ignorant intentions.

Arlee is The Miracle Worker, a teacher extraordinaire. We are, when it comes to our new pets, Helen Keller. And giving Helen her due, you haven't been challenged until you've tried to teach a 10-week old puppy to stop peeing on your living room carpet and chomping on your velvet couch and six-year old kid.

Arlee loves dogs, probably more than people. But she has laser beams for eyes and even the young pups know quickly who is in charge. When she commands "Sit," both puppies and owners hit the ground quickly. In the first class, she brings back six graduates and their masters to demonstrate that these mad little creatures can be turned into obedient, wonderful dogs. The six puppies, all about six months old, sit or lie next to their owners, do not bark, do not leap and squirm. They obey commands, walk quietly and demurely next to their owners, stay when told to stay. I am convinced that they are mechanical devices.

Arlee insists they are real and that our dogs too will behave like this after eight weeks of Puppy Kindergarten. "Yeah," I think to myself, "and my little Golden Retriever will move right on to Harvard by the fall."

Sunny, 14 weeks old, beautiful and sweet-natured, is turning my entire life upside down. "What was I thinking?" I keep repeating to myself at 5 a.m., while standing in my pajamas in the morning mist of my backyard as Sunny casually chews on a pine cone. I wanted Ben, my nine-year old son, to have a dog. Every boy should have a dog. It should be a fun dog, a big, friendly breed like a Golden, a dog you can run with and swim with and wrestle with on the floor.

But puppies are bad impulse buys. They are like infants with sharp teeth. They require constant attention and tireless energy. If you are not fully committed, you'll end up wanting to be committed…. to a sanitarium. If, like me, you don't have a partner or spouse to back you up, you will end up stressed, incoherent and desperate. It occurred to me, somewhere during the second week, that you ought to be able to rent puppies, play with them, and then bring them back at the end of the day.

And though Ben adores the puppy and pitches in as much as he can, I am the Alpha leader in this house and that means Sunny views me as the dominant member of the pack. In that role, I have to be constant and vigilant. Consistency is key. Puppies are willing to be molded if you ply them with enough tough love and liver treats. But getting them to sit and getting them to stop tearing your house to shreds are two different things.

In Arlee's classroom, the canine-challenged listen intently. Arlee takes the leash of Chelsea, a particularly agitated little Golden Retriever, and brings her to the center of the room. Without uttering a word, Arlee looks into the puppy's eyes, firmly handles the puppy's head and shoulders, and within 60 seconds, the squirming critter is lying calmly at her side.

"Can you come live at my house?" I want to ask Arlee. But she assures us that we can work this miracle too. She gives us lessons in basic obedience training. She helps us try to understand what the world looks like from the eyes of a puppy standing six inches off the ground. She assures us that barring the rare congenitally deformed dog, all of these animals are simply clay waiting to be molded into pets.

At the end of the class, Sunny sits at one end of the room. I walk to the opposite end, call her name, and she races to me, stops at my feet, and sits. I give her a treat as my classmates cheer their approval. Ben, Sunny, and I walk out into the steamy night to the car. For a bright shining moment, I feel hope. I remember the Jerry Seinfeld routine, about how aliens watching humans walking their dogs and cleaning up their poop would have no doubt who was the master race on this planet. Only six more classes to go until graduation. ❏

# At The Altar, For The Second Time Round

This Sunday, at the crest of the morning, I will take a new bride and turn an old life in a new direction. Though this is nothing at all like the life I had long ago believed I would have, it is wondrous still in the sheer unexpected beauty of the second chance.

What you think of all this is generally governed by the place from which you observe it. If you married young and fashioned a long, solid, and sustained life together, this may seem foreign as the shores of Greenland. If, on the other hand, you have had a bouncing life, like me, then you will appreciate the long distance we sometimes have to go to come back the shortest way correctly.

Second marriages are no big deal in a society that long ago accepted divorce as a spectator sport. One must hurry along to the fourth or fifth betrothal before anyone even blinks an eye. And yet, as I make my way back to matrimony after eight years of a single life, I can't help but feel the slightest nudge of a miracle here. I feel as if I've escaped from the "Relationships" section of the bookstore; leaping from the shelves of American angst into the very real beauty of a very real love.

I feel amazement at the clarity of this moment, so different from the first time around, at age 24, when I didn't know enough to turn the light up brighter and ask myself more questions. I feel remarkably lucky, after other doomed relationships and the imbalance of a single life, to have found Janie, this beautiful woman who willingly leaped in to not only become my life partner but my best friend.

And though we have had our share of relationship trauma since we first met on a cold winter night in the herbal remedies aisle at Debra's Natural Gourmet, we have weathered our storms with the wisdom born from head-knocking years of real life. In our collective cupboards, we have stored the joy and sorrow and strength of a lifetime's travails, the kind of experience not available to 24-year-olds. It's not about having diminished expectations, but rather it's about embracing the passion with a comfortable cloak of honesty and self-reliance. It is about discovering the difference between real love and co-dependence and holding each other with joy, not desperation.

Still, I will admit to some butterflies as Sunday approaches. Moving my T-shirt collection from half the dresser, emptying half the closet, noting the feminine items that now stock the bathroom vanity, have made me pause for just a moment. It is hard to describe what it feels like to establish a life alone and then shatter it with the infusion of another person's belongings, another person's quirks, another person's aura. Mixed in with the utter romance of it all is a very small voice saying, "Are you sure you know what you are doing here?"

And, in fact, I do know what I am doing here. It is, to me, the culmination of a lifetime search for this very person who will stand beside me on Sunday morning. It is not about destiny or fate or instant karma. It is being lucky enough to find out that you can travel to there and back again and actually hook up with your soul mate in a lasting and forever embrace. It is about finding out that there really is magic in a world that has so often felt without stardust and moonlight.

For me, the excitement of this wedding lies in all the silly, romantic trappings that we use to legalize the partnership. I am a sucker for wedding music and flowers and the beautiful wise words of the minister or rabbi or justice of the peace. I already feel the pulsing emotion of standing before cherished family and wonderful friends, with my 10-year-old son as my best man, while this sacred tradition plays out, this time for me and my bride. I've already gotten teary-eyed a dozen times just thinking about the day and the moment.

I cannot predict the future beyond Sunday morning. Yes, we will fly off to Bermuda for our honeymoon. And then we will return and settle into the life that happens after the final kiss, violin music and closing credits. There will be bills to pay and children (two of hers, one of mine) to attend to. And there will inevitably be giant potholes in the road ahead, most that we will steer nimbly around, some that we won't even see until we hit them. But this time around, there will be stardust and moonlight and the intoxicating reward of another chance taken.  ❑

# The Touch of an Island in Maine

My wife's family has vacationed on a pristine, elemental island off the coast of Maine for many decades. This island, with its rocky shoreline, stands of spruce, and lush, open meadows above the sea, is a quiet summer haven far from the madding crowd. I'm not allowed to tell its name or its exact location because its secluded and private nature is the essence of its allure.

As more and more people discover the Maine coastline, the little island seems to be attracting more uninvited guests who land their boats and hike on the island's trails. No one in the group of families who have long visited the island wants to be inhospitable. But to lose the quiet, undisturbed beauty of this place would be a cause for real sadness.

This tiny island has no roads, no cars, no electricity or plumbing, no toilets or showers or full-time residents. It is a speck of quiet solitude where bald eagles soar over the treetops and the sound of the lobster boats chugging out to the traps echoes through the early morning mist. It is a place where candlelight paints the dusk over games of Scrabble in the 180-year old farmhouse where people stay. It is a back-step in time where all the rhythms of life slow perceptibly and you can sit all day in the forgiving Maine sun, reading a novel without guilt or remorse.

My wife brought me to this place of her childhood summers for the first time in July. She fretted for weeks that I would be miserable without my bathroom and color TV. She prepped me about Cousin Martha, the infamous outhouse that serves the needs of however many guests might be in attendance. She made sure I brought lots of books and magazines and then held her breath as we motored across an inlet in an open launch toward the island's dock.

Though she was not exaggerating the rustic environment, my wife had no cause to worry. I really am not the suburban wuss she took me for. I'd used an outhouse or two in my day. I've slept in a tent and toasted marshmallows around a campfire with the best of them. In fact, I was not so much surprised or perturbed by anything on the island as I was enveloped by its serene integrity.

I had always hoped and believed that places like this still existed in this cacophonous world. I have long chafed at the reality that there are simply way too many people on this planet, pushing and shoving, needing and taking, demanding and grabbing the littlest space we have left. What could be more invigorating than a break from this new millennium world of digitized noise, traffic jams and rushes back and forth through the gates of modern life?

There are things in every life that are difficult to put down. These things perch on our shoulders and carouse in our brains day and night. They not only shape the view but often become the lens through which we see the world. As I rested against the giant boulders that form the island's shoreline, I focused on the very distinct movements of the ocean, the cormorants, the gulls and the small crabs in a nearby tidal pool. I tried to put the other stuff down, even for these too short moments in a too short summertime.

I had been overwhelmed before I got there with a burdensome work project, with financial worries, with news of suicide bombings in the Middle East and children being killed and a host of trouble in places I'd never been. I wondered if all this pain would disappear if I simply didn't see a newspaper or watch a television newscast for a week. I wondered if I could put it all down as easily as I would pick it back up when I returned to my real world.

And in truth, I don't really know how close I came to what I wanted. For a moment, up on the rocks with the ocean waves slamming against the shore, I had the sensation of being swallowed by the china blue sky. I listened to the call of an osprey whose nest was so near that she circled overhead and warned me away. I believed at that moment that if I could stay in this spot on this island for a long, long time, I could learn to inhale the magic scent of the raw ocean and that it could hold all the dreadful world at bay.

And now, with weeks gone by and the world's madness and beauty once again tainting every breath, the island recedes into photo albums and cocktail talk about summer vacations. What is left is the residue of this island dream; the sound a seagull makes or the wind in the rigging of a small boat lying at anchor. What is left is the remote sense of balance that is offered by just knowing such a place is ever there.  ❑

# Summertime and the Beads of Sweat

I took my son to day camp this morning and knew, as we drove along the shaded green length of Pope Road, that the summer had finally arrived in all the official glory of this unique season. The early morning air is still cool, but the hint of the afternoon heat is already on my skin. The lush smells of the roadside trees and overgrown fields pour into the car window with the unmistakable signals of summer. After 30 years in the Boston area, the distinct sensuality of a New England summer returns like an old friend who visits and lights your heart.

Even when nothing in your life is the same as before, summer imposes itself and demands attention. You can't ignore the slowing of the machinery that has its stranglehold on our lives. There are fewer cars clogging the rotary, men with downtown haircuts are playing with their small children at Emerson playground on weekday mornings, tour buses fill the parking lot near the Old North Bridge. Late at night, the stillness of the summer air—a blanket of humidity from a blistering day—is interrupted by woods sounds of cicadas and bullfrogs. The mosquitoes, especially bad this year (and every year), lie in wait to ambush anyone brave or foolish enough to walk in the dusky evening.

This summer, however, the living isn't so easy for a lot of people in New England and around the country. After several years of mind-numbing growth and prosperity, harsh economic reality has not so much settled back in as simply dropped like an anvil from the sky. "Whack, whack, whack" is the sound you hear: jobs being chopped, retirement funds plummeting, energy prices soaring, hearts beating just a tiny bit faster as the anxiety levels rise with the heat.

This downturn feels odd, different than others in the past. The swiftness and harshness of the fall from grace has left ambiguity mixed in with the pain. There is little evidence that real hardship has settled in. Airplanes are still filled with cramped travelers, the shopping malls remain crowded, the air of prosperity has hardly diminished in towns like Concord, Acton, Wellesley or Lincoln.

But the numbers don't lie, and it is now hard to find anyone who doesn't know someone who's been laid off from their job. It is hard to believe that anyone of moderate means hasn't been impacted by the downturn. So many of us invested what savings we had in mutual funds tied to the equities markets. One look at the monthly retirement fund statement and it becomes harder and harder to justify that dream vacation you planned last fall or the new car you thought you might buy this year.

The domino effect seems to have kicked in: trouble in one industry sector spilling into another and then another even as the pundits claim that things will get better soon. Though many agree with the President that a tax cut is in order, few believe in the laughable prospect that a $300 rebate check is going to change anyone's life or jumpstart the struggling economy. That check might just cover a month's electric bill this summer, but barely.

In truth, the economy is simply teetering. It hasn't decided yet whether to settle back down or tumble into the abyss. The growing uncertainty and the prolonged stretch of negative earnings news from corporate America—particularly the bellwether technology sector—just adds to the anxiety levels.

There is, however, a response that is appropriate in the summertime. We can hunker down, tighten our belts, and ride it out like flinty old New Englanders have always done. Those summer thunderstorms that blacken the sky and send streaks of lightening and thunder boomers bellowing across the heavens can wreak havoc on a day at the beach or a night at Fenway Park. But most people find beauty and awestruck wonder just sitting by a window or leaning against the car in the garage and watching these storms pass in their full fury. We can ride out the economic storm the same way.

My wife and I have decided to simplify by staying home, skipping an elaborate vacation trip, and finding joy in localizing our summer. We'll take the dog for long walks in the woods, head for the beach, take on a long-awaited project around the house, work in the garden, barbecue with friends and find utter joy in reading a good book or going for an early morning run.

In fact, there is something intensely liberating about letting the summer wash over you like a late day rain shower. Every day we can remember how much we anticipated this season on those endlessly cold winter days. We can revel in the enveloping warmth and long, luscious days when the sun doesn't want to set. Economists will tell you this is the wrong response; we should keep on spending and spending to keep the economic engine humming. Those same economists never did explain how to spend what you no longer have.

There has always been something primitive about the summer, a season of passion and heat. Perhaps that makes it the best time of all to return to our own internal greenhouses and ease back on the throttle of consumption. There may be lessons learned in the summer gardens that have nothing to do with tomatoes and cucumbers. ❑

# The Dads Go to Camp

I lay on a blue air mattress in a tiny tent in a wide green field. In the tent to my left, a mere arm's length away, a stranger began to snore like a gas-powered leaf blower. In my tent, my 13-year old son also began to snore, somehow in lockstep with the stranger. I recalled my favorite Three Stooges episodes in which the hapless trio inevitably shared a small bed and snored in harmonious chorus. "Ah," I sighed as sleep drifted further away into the rain-soaked Berkshire night.

It was Dad's Weekend at Camp Becket, a century old boys camp in Becket, Mass., and I knew as I lay awake in this wondrous, birch-filled setting, that sleep was a small price to pay for this 48-hour salute to quality time. These Becket folks had been luring fathers out to the Berkshires for 80 summers and had obviously observed how transformative the time could be for boys and their dads. Here, there were no computers, no widescreen TVs, no Red Sox or Yankee games, no movies, and no mothers to suggest dinner out at the Olive Garden. If you put a boy and his father together, eliminate the distractions, offer up a perfect setting, and supply the food and canoe paddles, something magical is likely to happen.

I arrived early on Friday afternoon, armed with sleeping bags, a heavily-laden duffle and industrial-sized bug repellent. My brush with nature usually involved an hour of the Discovery Channel so this weekend in the wilderness would likely be a test of wills. Camping is not a natural inclination for my tribe. I bought a mosquito-net head covering that one wears over a hat. Donning it, one bears a striking resemblance to the Grim Reaper. My son undoubtedly wouldn't allow me to wear it outside the tent.

Nonetheless, feeling confident, even a bit cocky, I set up the tent in record time and went off to find Ben. It had rained most of the day and a misty fog had settled over the lake. Out there somewhere, Ben was fishing. As I stood gazing out at the water, I realized that I had no memories like this, having never gone to summer camp as a child. I planned to call my mother and complain when I got home.

I wandered near the boys' cabins as more fathers began to arrive. I'd worried that the weekend would be competitive: three-legged races, pancake eating contests, tree-climbing amid the pines. I had envisioned all the other fathers looking like Jason Giambi. I'd have no chance. But I was soon rid of that delusion. The other fathers looked more or less like me, and I would probably not spend the weekend in the infirmary. Besides, the setting was so peaceful and bucolic that there seemed little chance for this to devolve into a test of testosterone.

Ben spotted me before I saw him. He raced up the dirt path, his face beaming, and gave me a long hug. Though it had only been three weeks since we'd seen each other, we both realized this was the longest we'd ever been apart. It is hard to measure the full thrill of seeing your boy, tanned and tousle-haired, after a long absence. I held onto him for an extra moment. "Come on," I finally said through misty eyes. "Let's bring the rest of the stuff to the tent."

Without a lot of fanfare, the dads arrived and slipped into their sons' routines, the camp activities that become sainted memories of childhood. Some of us chased Frisbees, others practiced archery, still others did picturesque belly flops from the dock into the lake. We ate in the spacious dining hall, our sons serving us as waiters, and sang along to "B-B-B-Becket in the Berkshires," one of the camp's countless anthems. I was tempted to leap onto a table and start singing Allen Sherman's old classic, "Hello Muddah, Hello Faddah," but Ben gave me the look.

Ben's counselors, teenagers not much older than he, snagged us into a wild game of Ultimate Frisbee in the dusk. We ended up sweaty and laughing for the final nightly activity, Cabin Chat. In the darkness of the cabin, dimly lit by a single candle, eight campers and eight dads lay in their sons' bunks as Jamie, Ben's counselor from Edinburgh, Scotland, began the evening discussion. "What was the highlight of your day?" he asked. Ben's friend Ian spoke first.

"The highlight of my day was seeing my dad when he arrived at camp," he said. "I realized how much I missed him and was really happy he was here." Each boy had a turn. They all said about the same thing. What was clear was that they were not simply copying each other, as adolescent boys will often do. There were no wrong answers here.

The fathers got an opportunity as well. I could feel the emotion as all of us echoed our sons, sitting side by side, arms around each other.

I finally fell asleep that night on my air mattress, a couple of restless hours interrupted by a crystal clear dawn. I dragged Ben out of his sleeping bag for a pre-breakfast canoe trip around the lake. I thought about how much you learn about your own son when you put yourself in strange, beautiful places together and just admire the person he has become. If they'd only let me sing "Kumbaya", the weekend would have been perfect. ❏

# Bringing Home the Lost Boys

Sometimes, the most amazing stories are right under our noses, but we just don't see them. Here and across America are the lost boys, a legion of young men out of high school, college, drifting, sometimes aimlessly, sometimes close to the shore, in lives that somehow, sometime disconnected and set them in a depressing spiral to nowhere.

They are in your town, every town, and they are the sons of your friends, your cousins, your siblings, your colleagues at work and yourselves. Each has an individual story but the results are stunningly similar. They live at home or in cramped apartments where the social circle spins around alcohol and drugs. They work at jobs which hold little or no allure and little or no future, paying just enough to keep a car on the road and beer in the refrigerator.

Some look at them as trapped in a time warp, unable to leave high school behind, hanging with the same crowd, mired in empty friendships that reach their peak in drinking games on Friday nights in someone's tiny living room or at keggers in large suburban homes when the parents are out of town.

I had always known about the lost boys, at least vaguely, because in some ways, things have not changed all that much since I was that age a long time ago. Every generation has its lost boys who never quite catch the brass ring, never find the right girl to marry, or a job good enough to fund a reasonable chance, let alone a hopeful future.

Yet now, it just feels like there are more lost boys than before. My stepson Cameron brought that world back vividly into my own over the past few years. When his mom and I started dating, Cameron was an unhappy 16-year old, resentful of my presence, angry at the absence of his real father, and on a journey into drinking and drugs that formed the arc of his high school years. He tried college, but a dormitory life for him was like putting the wolf's bed, computer, and school supplies into the henhouse. Most of the two semesters were spent in an alcoholic haze.

After he dropped out, he tried living with his father in New Jersey, took on one or two dead-end jobs and slipped further into his own private oblivion. When he drank, he drank hard, a classic binge drinker who believed the goal was to drink until he passed out. The occasional visit with us brought him back to his high school buddies, some of whom were equal to his abilities, the others unable or unwilling to say anything to stop him.

And when he hit bottom, passed out on a street near Boston, taken into protective custody by the local police on the eve of a family vacation to Florida, Cameron had an epiphany, and so did we. We offered our help, a place to live, a place with love and support but an excuse-free zone. He admitted to his alcoholism, went into a rehab program, found a job, and slowly, sometimes painfully, began a new journey.

In a world cluttered with sad endings, Cameron reached deep inside and grabbed onto an inner strength and resolve that surprised us and probably him. He stopped drinking and hasn't faltered. Even surrounded by the friends whose habits never changed, he remained steadfast. Through suddenly clear eyes, he began to see how boring and empty that lifestyle was and always would be. He still had an entire life ahead of him and something better: another chance.

Cameron is smart, very smart. He is big and strong and fiercely devoted. He loves children and understood in a moment of great clarity that he might just make an incredible teacher. This fall, he will start college again. He has already aced two of the three classes he was required to take to get accepted, and when he returns to the classroom full-time in September, he will be present and purposeful.

My wife and I don't know how all this will play out. It is mostly unknowable. But what we see is an amazing young man, spirited, feisty, intensely loyal to his sister and stepbrother, a lover of animals with a gentle and kind soul. He chafes at living at home, and we understand that and think it is good. Still, we love having him around us and present in our lives.

As the old spiritual goes, he once was lost, like the others, but now he is found, within himself and within the world. And in that is a message of hope to anyone who knows another lost boy. Go find him and bring him home.  ❏

# Thoreau's Backyard

Sunday morning breakfast at the Colonial Inn. Omelettes, fresh coffee, croissants, and homemade waffles. The smell of the bacon and maple syrup drift across the air like gustatory sirens.

There is no possible way to sit in these rooms and not feel the weight of a different time and the gathering of voices that reside in the walls and ancient floorboards. If there are ghosts, they are present, lined up in period costumes from long ago days when the sound of horses' hooves clip-clopped past diners on ancient mornings.

Outside, the summer air is heavy with the humidity of early August and the certainty of later rain. The heaviness begets a stillness, anticipation of a breeze that doesn't come. The sound of riders, resting by their bicycles on the common, moves along toward the veranda, literal as something just short of words.

My friends from New York express their admiration for this sacred spot, visiting for the first time and getting breakfast and a taste of this small, remarkable town, in one sitting. I have brought others to this place for maiden visits, and the response is always the same. Yet I never tire of hearing the newborn admiration as if they were praising my child.

There is something both odd and rejuvenating about living in a destination. Here, in Thoreau's backyard, we dwell on the edge of taking it all for granted, but never get quite beyond that moment of surprise or pride or irony or wonder. This Old North Bridge could have been anywhere really and yet it is here, fording this river and these hallowed banks where a million ghosts really do reside and stamp their approval at this notion of never forgetting.

I myself came from far away, both geographically and emotionally, to touch such a small town and make contact. It is this collection of names and faces and places that are simply my own snapshot in the continuum. Who will remember this Sunday morning in a hundred years on this porch in the hot summer of tomorrow? Will locals parade around in the shorts and t-shirts of our day to commemorate a new ancient time?

We walk along the street with bunting and bricks and the incongruities of tying past to present. We look at notices of $3 million homes in realty office windows and reach out to touch the dates and names on the ancient markers in the shade of a mid-town graveyard.

There is the temptation to lie down flat in the green grass and close one's eyes and feel the sanctity of this ground. We almost never do. We almost always keep walking with the surety that the next visit will afford new luxuries of time and space.

In the bookstore window, there is a display of the new works of an author who will read his words that very afternoon. Inside, the dark mahogany shelves are lined with thousands of books that form an irresistible lure to those who love words or browsing or the smell of bookshops on summer mornings. Stories in books, stories on the sidewalk, stories floating across the centuries. So many writers stopped here to form their words. So many still do.

I very rarely grow philosophical about my visits from home to the center of town. There is always a task or a meeting or simply somewhere else to go. There is a larger world of continents and politicians and oceanic skies that always intrude and block perspective. There is always so much to think about, to hear about, to do.

And yet, when my friends are ready to drive away, back to their own places, their own homes, their own green lawns, I hand them this memory of a visit to a small town whose church bells pierce the hot summer air. I wish them a safe journey and a last quick glance and I invite them to come back, with all their belongings, to stay forever.

And they laugh, not at the absurdity but at the sheer wonder of such an idea. Who would not want to live right here, smile at familiar faces, walk through distinct streets with perfect houses and shade trees and dreams?

When the rain finally arrives, it is strong and draws hissing steam from the overheated streets. The luscious mid-summer greens grow wet and verdant, and the white clapboard and fences are almost luminous against the darkening sky. I have the urge to leave my car behind the camera shop and walk off breakfast in the miles to Walden. Walden is just a pond, like Concord is just a town. And I am not the last one who wishes he could walk along this road forever. ❏

# Fall

The pumpkins rise like an orange mountain at Arena Farms as we flash down Rt. 2 in the Saab. On October Saturday mornings like this one, the sky is so blue that it shines like wet paint. I had driven out on this highway thirty years before, when I was still in college, and places like Concord felt like the far end of the world. Living in a dorm in Kenmore Square back then, Boston was big enough to contain my dreams. But on this drive, we headed out on Rt. 2 to the west and it was October and the leaves were in full fire, brilliant and spectacular and surreal. And for some reason, I can never drive down this highway in the autumn without remembering this single ride out into the countryside, speeding toward my own future. ❏

# The Glamour of the Writer's Life

One of the great misconceptions is that of the writer's life. To the public, the writer is a glamorous figure, a celebrity of pen and ink and insight who lives an envious life, a life of imagination, cocktail parties, and travel to exotic places.

Unlike movie stars and sports heroes, writers are mysteriously alluring, intriguing in their ability to find things out, weave lives out of words, and illuminate places that were once dark.

Writers are cerebral and cool, good to have at parties, inevitably hip in whatever changing cycles popular culture directs itself. Even in an era of plunging book sales and the Internet, even when no one allegedly has the time or desire to read anymore, there stands the writer, who understands viscerally what John Corry, a former New York Times reporter, said. "Each day I wrote defined me. In a society where so many ache to be heard, a byline was better than money."

I keep that comment by Corry in my office next to my computer. More often than you might believe, I glance at those words to reaffirm why I am sitting in that solitary space, tapping at those plastic keys, knee-deep in this glamorous life.

And any writer worth his or her salt could not help but be moved by the suicide death of Anthony Lukas, the brilliant but tortured writer whose new book, "Big Trouble," is just being released this month. Lukas, a former New York Times reporter, two-time Pulitzer Prize winner, author of the award-winning chronicle of Boston's busing crisis "Common Ground," killed himself in June. At 64, he was another writer dying well before his time, tortured by the personal demon of depression that haunted him most of his life.

It would be foolish hyperbole to suggest that Lukas's suicide was a "writer's thing." Clearly, Lukas had lost a long and anguished battle with depression that his friends trace back to his mother's suicide when Lukas was just 8 years old. In his professional life, he became a perfectionist, driven well beyond the bounds of reason to track the details, get every last fact just right, to avoid any and all mistakes. He spent eight years on his last book, countless solitary hours chasing minute facts and details, spiraling downward in his despair that whatever he produced would never be good enough.

And yet writers, even the most mentally healthy and balanced of us, do, in fact, understand Lukas's anguish. Concord, a town rich with a writing tradition, home to dozens of wonderful, successful writers both past and present, has undoubtedly been both a haven and a hell for the writer's singular experience.

Writing is, at its heart, among the loneliest of professions, hours and hours spent alone in front of a computer screen, tapping out our reason for being, hoping someone will read the words, be touched by our stories, laugh, cry, or just smile with a nod of recognition. Writing is, at its heart, a giant ego trip for those too shy to go on stage, too clumsy to slug homeruns, too presumptuous to keep our thoughts and opinions to ourselves. In a world where so many ache to be heard, writing is the salve to that ache. But it comes with a price.

Will it be good enough, we ask ourselves? Will we be questioned for our accuracy, our style, our insight? Will we be ridiculed, poorly reviewed, lambasted by critics or, worst of all, ignored completely?

Because of all that solitary time—after the interviews and road trips and phone calls are completed—we need the feedback, demand the response, breathe in that rush of contact with our audience. Writers feign detachment and aloofness, but for an author, a scathing review can send some to bed for a week. Like small children, we yearn for approval, a kind word, a belief that all that alone time was worthwhile. We emerge from work on a lengthy article, a screenplay, a manuscript, like bears from a winter's hibernation, grouchy, hungry, in need of some honey.

Most writers never know fame or fortune. We write because it is a calling, like playing the piano or running long distances. And we endure the solitude and the self-doubt to reach for that one sentence that sings or rings true, to give voice to a unique thought, a moment of clouds and rain and inspiration.

For writers like Lukas, or Michael Dorris or Sylvia Plath, no amount of approval or praise can be enough. As Arthur Gelb,

Lukas's editor at the New York Times, said, "He felt that writing was his vacation from living." We can only give ourselves solace in the words they leave behind and be grateful that beauty can indeed co-exist with pain.  ❏

# Farewell to the Walking Lady

"Concord is the walking lady, sturdy strides along Harrington, backpack full but not over-full, face set and determined that there are miles to go today and more tomorrow."

I wondered when I wrote these words in my last Journal column whether the walking lady would see them and know that I was talking about her, including her high up on my list of images that evoked the town for me.

There is nothing but sadness and lasting irony that I only just learned the walking lady's name now, after five years, because of a horrible tragedy. Caroline DePledge was killed last week in the crash of Swissair Flight 111 along with her husband Norman and two grown children, Jane and Michael. They were among 229 passengers and crew members who perished aboard the flight to Geneva when the plane plunged into the sea off Halifax, Nova Scotia.

I had had a million questions for Caroline DePledge. I saw her nearly every day for the five years I lived in West Concord. She did nothing more than walk, but hers was not a casual stroll now and again; she was the walking lady. She walked everywhere, constantly, winter, summer, spring, and fall, a backpack strapped on. She walked in the morning and in the afternoon, in sunshine and in storms. She walked with passion, if such a thing is possible.

I never knew her destination but she clearly had one. I never met her formally but we came to the point where we waved to each other and said hello. She always smiled, the smile of a person who gardens and has inner peace and a life with a center. Walking was not a burden or a drudgery. She embraced her path and let her hard, muscled legs carry her without complaint.

And though she walked alone a good deal of the time, Caroline DePledge had a walking man as well. I assumed it was her husband, though I had no names to put to the faces. Seeing the two together only added to the mystery, to the allure of these people I knew but didn't know.

Because when they walked together, the walking lady and walking man were one. They were clearly in their late 50s or perhaps early 60s, yet they walked together like young lovers. They held hands sometimes, but often they had their arms around each other's waists, pulled close, deep in conversation and oblivious to the road and the trees and the passing cars.

That they adored each other was not lost on anyone who saw them. I could only watch them and envy this bond that is so simple and beautiful and profound, and wonder why I never saw anyone else in my neighborhood walking together this way. Who are these people, I always wondered? Where are they going? What is their story and their inspiration? Do they ever realize how good they make me feel, just to see them together, walking in love this way?

And in the way that life becomes a collage of the things you see and experience everyday, of family, friends, trees in the yard and the morning sun, roads familiar and well-traveled, the DePledges had been woven into mine.

When I heard about the Swissair crash, I had the usual reaction. This catastrophe, like other airline crashes, had been horrible and ghastly but impersonal in the way tragedies are, in this media age. I could understand the pain of the relatives and friends of the many victims, but it was distant and muted in the way that such great disasters always are. But when I read in the Globe about the family from West Concord who had died in the crash and heard the description of the lady who loved to walk because she didn't drive a car, my heart sank.

I drove over to Blue Jay Drive, hoping to see the walking lady along the way, perhaps striding down Rt. 62 toward the Stop & Shop or arm in arm with her husband on Old Stow Rd. I stopped and asked a neighbor who confirmed my worst fears, that I'd finally learned the walking lady's name, and it was too late to ask her all my questions or offer my admiration.

I stopped in front of the quiet and empty house where the beautiful perennial beds were ablaze with the flowers that Caroline DePledge had tended. I felt the loss of a friend and a profound grief flowed over me even though we'd never formally met. I knew that Concord, for me, would always be the walking lady, smiling, determined, forever at peace, with miles to go today and more tomorrow. ❏

# A Father, Now Twenty Years Gone

The phone rang at 1 a.m. on a long ago October night. When I heard my mother's voice, strained and breaking, I knew that my father had died. My mother lied to me, saying he'd suffered another heart attack and that he was in the hospital. She told me to hurry home, which was a four-hour car ride from Boston to New Jersey, and she hung up before I could say anything else.

It was that kind of surreal moment when the pain is building somewhere off center in your brain but hasn't yet hit. I remember the sensation of trying to catch my breath, searching for oxygen in a room suddenly airless and suffocating. I remember talking to my wife, now awake and reaching for the light; telling her what had happened even though I had no confirmation of my fears.

This was the phone call I had been waiting for for a decade. Ten years earlier, at age 47, my father had suffered a serious heart attack. I was 16 and everything I had believed about my world up till then had changed forever. My father had been a block of granite, the foundation of my life and my family's life. He was quiet and strong and impervious to the forces of nature. Family, friends, strangers responded to his reassuring presence. If trouble arose, he was the one we called, all of us. His hands were thick and strong and could hold up a world.

But when his heart first failed him, and when he returned home pale and drained and clearly afraid, it made me understand that nothing would be the same again. I remember going into my room, closing the door and weeping uncontrollably for a long time. I remember the entrance into my life of the presence of death, waiting somewhere nearby, to emerge in the form of a phone call shattering the night.

We had another decade. I considered it a great gift. His eyes were always tired, but he got to see my sister get married and give birth to his first and second grandchildren. He got to see me off to college and to stand next to me at my own wedding. He never grew bitter or reclusive but lived a life surrounded by love and embraced by family. I never saw two people more in love than my father and mother, and that was a great gift that sustained my mother long after he was gone.

On October 6, it will be 20 years since my father died. John Irving, the novelist, once wrote, "When someone you love dies, you don't lose them all at once. You lose them in pieces, bit by bit over a long time." Thus it has been with my father. The intense pain, the heat of grief, has long since passed, though I remember those feelings well. But even now, I still feel the empty place where he was and wonder how our lives would have gone had he been alive all these years.

I think about how lost in myself I became, stricken with para-lyzing doubts about my career and my marriage and my seeming inability to find balance. I think about how he never seemed to have such doubts, though in hindsight I'm sure he had plenty. By age 22, he had flown 50 missions in a B-24 Liberator bomber during World War II. He left a diary from that time and talked about losing buddies in training missions, about surviving a raid over the oil fields of Ploesti, about his homesickness for his family. He had barely finished high school, but he came home from the war, opened a tiny jewelry shop in Manhattan across the street from Macy's, and made a good life.

That night that he died, I drove through the wet autumn darkness and felt as if I was floating outside the car with the wind and soft rain in my face. I remember the sensation of driving toward disaster, of the prospect of a funeral and facing my mother and sisters and brother, all bewildered and crazy with despair. I still hear the music that was playing on the car stereo.

My father revisits me every once in a while in my dreams. I've introduced him to my son, whom he never got to meet, and I touch his hand which is strong and thick as it ever was. I have made no plans for this anniversary which is no more or less than a reminder of the passage of time. I honor his place in my life every day – his picture hangs on my bedroom wall – so this isn't about tribute. I still feel his love coursing through me. His death taught me to celebrate the bond between me and my son and to never take a single moment for granted. If anything, he has been my greatest teacher all these years gone. ❑

# Running Into the Autumn Sun

I cannot wrap my arms around this pain.

I run through the crisp new autumn air sucking in breath, shielding my eyes from the early sun. This brilliant morning sun, so blinding in this season, burns my eyelids even as these tears fall behind my steps.

In this autumn morning, we go about our business.....some of us running in the often-empty hope that goodness will come from the sweat of our motion. You don't see any other creatures of the world inflicting such self-absorbed vanity upon themselves. Panthers don't run to shed excess pounds. Mockingbirds don't fly to tighten their abs.

We, the people, have created this illusion about life and death. We alone have the capacity to embrace the concept that life is a special vessel of hope and beauty. And we alone have the capacity to destroy the hope and beauty with our own hands. It is this dichotomy that makes us run.

I run through this dawn because the pain is more than I can bear. I have seen these terrible images on my television screen, over and over and over and over. I could feel a rip in the fabric of the universe, torn with the visceral heat of an exploding sky. It felt like all the noise collected in a single primal scream that arched across the naked sky. I could not watch and I could not look away.

We awakened, numb and shaken, to the awful truth of this dreadful morning: that our love of life cannot shut out the strident darkness. These things have existed side by side throughout the history of man in a mesmerizing lock step through the centuries, a sound of laughter drowned out by a cry of sorrow.

A friend calls and tells me that we now understand how people live in the rest of the world. We have been bathed in our own deep innocence, and now we are cold and shivering and wet with fear that a new kind of enemy has infiltrated our existence, and all bets are off. As I run through an early morning shadow, I ask myself if we can believe such a thing... and if it is true, can we live every day with such fear.

That horrible night, I held my son in my arms as we watched the images flicker ceaselessly across the screen. He is only 12 and has grown up in a world of media violence and reality TV and Internet connection. He told me that his heart was beating faster, and he felt shaky and weak. I tried to imagine what this moment would mean to a child in this kind of world. Despite all that he has seen that I had never seen at his age, he was still scared. What could I tell him to soothe his fears? We can never really learn to live in such a world. We can only push the fear aside as best we can and move ahead, slowly, tentatively, one step at a time.

But this time is different, and everyone can feel the difference. There will be no business as usual because time became still on that fateful morning. The clocks may have spun on and the cycles of the day kept turning, but time has halted and we turn, each of us, in a slow spiral of self-reflection and doubt. Who am I now, I ask myself? What will I become when time begins again?

As I race against the morning air, I weigh each footfall and listen to the sounds of my own breath and my own steps. I once ran with an effortless rhythm, with a certain balance engulfed in the natural flow of moving forward. Now the balance is almost gone, tilted toward the pain, leaning like a broken tower in the sky.

If only I can stand shoulder to shoulder with you and you and you, I will somehow regain my balance and we will hurdle this evil together on history's wings. On a given morning, not far from now, the sky will fill with angels and the screams of horror will become a chorus of wondrous voices singing loud. I know these voices are there; I can almost hear them now. I run towards them because there is nowhere else to run. ❏

# *Like No Other, a Time for Thanksgiving*

Shortly after the September 11th terrorist attacks, The New York Times created a new daily section called "A Nation Challenged." For two months, the section has carried detailed coverage of the aftermath of the attacks, the war against Al Qaeda and the Taliban, the anthrax outbreak, and the nation's attempt to come to grips with a tragedy of monstrous proportions. The last page of the section is devoted to the victims lost in the destruction of the World Trade Center.

Each day, the page has postage stamp-size photographs of about a dozen victims. Each is accompanied by a short description of that person and the lives they lived before disaster struck. They are firefighters, policemen, Wall Street workers, maintenance workers, emergency personnel. They are men and women, every race, creed, color. But thus far, the majority seem to be young, white men, mostly in their 20s, 30s, and 40s, the kind of demographic that fits for those at work in the economic heart of the city and the country.

It is difficult to look into these faces and read these stories. What is so stark and so unremittingly sad is the ordinariness of these lives. They are not famous or accomplished or extraordinary. They are us, you and me, just people who had begun an ordinary early September day, going to work, attending meetings, preparing reports, talking to clients. Many had left simple homes where they had risen, dressed, hugged their children, kissed their spouses goodbye. They had never for a single moment believed that this would be the last time they would do these things. They had all the hopes, anxieties, fears, excitement, cares and dreams that we all carry with us.

The idea that more than 3000 people were wiped out in a single violent act is nearly impossible to process. But seeing these tiny biographies, purposely written not to be obituaries but rather celebrations of a life, personalizes each story and sends out a wrinkle into the universe. If you could count how many people that your life touches and has touched, what number would you come up with? Would it be 20? 50? 1000? And if you multiply that number by 3000, you can only start to understand the concentric circles of this unspeakable tragedy that ripple out like a pebble thrown in a pond. You can begin to understand that there are not six degrees of separation at all, not even two or one. Somehow, we were all touched because we all dressed in the same cloak of the American experience.

The stories are too short to fill in the details. They are little more than implications. There are the small children, now motherless or fatherless, left to try to understand an empty space that will be with them for the rest of their lives. There are the wives or husbands, now alone, trying to imagine how they can get through the next night, the next week, the next month. There are brothers, sisters, mothers, fathers, friends, colleagues who have carried this ache in their hearts for two months and who know there will be no solace anytime soon.

126

We have all felt this disbelief as we've tried to reconcile the terror and return to some sense of normalcy, if not complacency. We have gotten on with our lives because there is nothing else that we can do. We try to comprehend this war and the juxtaposition of this new world with the one we watched disappear in the cloud of black smoke on September 11th. It is only two months and for most of us, there is more than a sense of unease. Grief cannot be hurried or willed away, which is why this Thanksgiving promises to be like no other in recent memory.

This year, I can give thanks from the deepest part of my soul. I have already found myself, in the darkest moments of the night, feeling what it would be like to lose my most precious loved ones in the blink of a tear-filled eye. What if it had been my wife, my children, my mother, my brother, my sisters on those planes, in those towers? What if it had been me? What if it had been you? In those 3000 stories, we are there, so close that we can feel the heartbreak of the empty chairs around the Thanksgiving table.

For those of us spared for no other reason than the confluence of time and place, the gratitude must be profound. If we've ever had a day to be truly thankful, let it be this Thanksgiving. It is so much easier to understand and appreciate what we have now, where we are now, how we live now, than ever before. This is the year to look into the eyes of those you love, to hold tighter than before, to pass the gravy and the stuffing and the essence of this life, and take nothing for granted. This is the year to hear the words of the song, "On and on, the rain will fall like tears from a star. On and on, the rain will sing, how fragile we are, how fragile we are." ❏

# *When a Daughter Leaves for College*

My step-daughter just left for college. She spent the summer embracing her friends and tearing away from a life that has been her platform for 18 years. This is a wrenching time, as anyone who has sent a child off to college knows too well. In the days leading up to her departure, my wife often broke out in tears for no apparent reason. But of course, there was a reason and this monumental separation is painful and emotional and filled with tears and sighs and pangs of sadness.

You'd have to see and feel the love between these two to understand how majestic this moment truly is. Perhaps you've seen it in your own homes and, if so, you are very lucky. My wife and her daughter flow together like parallel rivers, coursing along, often twisting across and through each other, rushing with each other's rhythms and pulses.

They are tall and beautiful and feed each other's souls with a lifetime of nourishment that is as strong as a redwood and as steady as a heartbeat. Though my step-daughter is off to college and at the gatehouse to her own adult life, I know that these two will never truly separate. Whether she ends up living in Paris or next door, she will remain a part of her mother's being, like a limb.

The anguish of this time is ameliorated by the joy and amazement of seeing a child becoming a young woman right before our eyes.

We know we will miss her deeply. We will miss her presence that lights up a room, her laughter, her wit and wisdom, her compassion and her burgeoning confidence that the world is waiting and she must go out into it.

We will not miss her messy room and messier bathroom. Or perhaps we will, after all, on a somber winter afternoon when the house is just a shade quieter than before and snow is falling on a gray yard. One can never estimate the subtractions in a life and how they will fill in or not fill in.

For me, this parting is different from my wife's but no less emotional. I came very late into this child's life and for a long time, was not a welcome participant. There are volumes written about the difficulties of merging families, and they are all accurate and insightful. But books cannot convey the sense of alienation and distance that we experienced for so long. I felt like I was standing at the locked door of an exclusive club. I could hear the party going on inside, but I was not going to get past the bouncers.

The efforts I made were mostly received with coldness and a seeming indifference. I was not welcome, and her determination to keep it that way was stiffened by her own sense of dread that she could not make me disappear completely. Clearly she was not happy that this unwanted stranger was taking up space in her mother's life....space that belonged to her.

Just before our wedding, she told her mom and me that it would be "the worst day of my life." Her smiles, she warned, were just a front hiding her sadness.

What could I say or do? Her mother and I were determined to be together. She would come around, hopeful friends would say. It will take time, they counseled.

Strangely, my love for her had been forming all along. I could see close up this remarkable person, so sweet and caring to everyone, excluding me. If a change ever did happen, it would be worth the wait.

I really couldn't say what happened. We had an apocalyptic episode after a family vacation. She spilled her unhappiness out in a torrent, and I decided to shut down and offer silence and distance. After that, things began to change. Slowly, slowly, like two dancers in a strange tango.

You can analyze and deconstruct everything in life, but in the end, I believe in love, totally and without exception. There was simply too much of it in our collective hearts to keep this fire burning. Somewhere, at some point, most of the defenses finally fell. Steady, relentless caring and support helped. Her own growing up helped even more. The metamorphosis was amazing to her mother and to me. The embrace, while tentative at times, was real and in the long run, the struggle ceased, replaced by something new and special. I'm sure that I cannot feel that incredible bond that her mother feels for her. But I'm not all that far away anymore.

So as she leaves for college, I find myself misty-eyed and aching with that same feeling of separation. She has, in an incredibly short time, become my own daughter in my heart. And after we unloaded her things from the car, carried them up to the dorm room, helped her get settled, and then prepared to drive home, I shared a good cry with my wife and then smiled at the very thought of our girl, off and on her own. ❏

# More Fog from Another War

In the powerful Academy Award-winning documentary *The Fog of War*, former secretary of defense Robert McNamara wells up with tears and admits that he made a disastrous mistake in advocating the escalation of the Vietnam War during the 1960s. More than anything, McNamara was haunted by the tragedy of an administration that sent nearly 60,000 American soldiers to die in an unwinnable war.

History has always been the ultimate classroom, the arena in which we either learn from our mistakes or are doomed to repeat them. And that is why it is not difficult, for those of us old enough to remember, to realize how remarkably similar things suddenly feel today with this current administration and this war in Iraq.

Whatever political agenda one might adhere to, it is impossible not to feel the agony of watching our soldiers struggle in a military quagmire with no end in sight and seemingly no clear cut plan for success from the administration that set the war in motion. As the death toll mounts and the images from the frontlines become more and more horrifying, Americans across the nation are growing increasingly restless with a president who doesn't have any answers beyond a pledge to "stay the course."

This is not an acceptable response, and it is not surprising that our nation is once again divided along political and philosophical lines. One can easily find a parallel to the days of Vietnam, when our country was angrily divided between those who opposed the war and those who supported President Richard Nixon and his unwavering commitment to the doomed Vietnam War.

Four years ago, I strayed from my usual writing in this column to comment on George W. Bush and his credentials, or lack thereof, to be president of the United States. I was appalled that this man was the best the Republican Party could offer as a candidate and even more appalled at the way the election played out. I envisioned the disaster a Bush presidency might bring, but I had no idea of the magnitude of this disaster. I caught a lot of flak from local Republicans who disagreed with my views. My belief remains that one of the tenets of the greatness of America is our freedom of speech and our ability to enthusiastically disagree with our politicians and each other and engage in a discourse about matters of consequence.

Back then, some questioned whether this was appropriate material for a local paper where most turned for news of school board meetings and local elections. To me, the ramifications of the decisions made by politicians in Washington are always felt most acutely in the small cities and towns of our nation where the soldiers come from. It is in these places where the names of the casualties have faces; where these soldiers had lives and people who knew them and loved them. It is in these places where the tragedy of miscalculated decisions by a misguided administration becomes real. So it is appropriate to write about this in a local paper.

What I presume all my fellow citizens, in small towns to big cities, want to know is where are we going under this president's guiding hand? In a remarkably short time, by history's standards, President Bush has managed to turn a just and reasonable response to terrorism into a global disaster for the United States. Urged on by his advisors, this president has alienated our friends with his "My way or the highway" cowboy posturing and further inflamed an already hostile Arab world into a level of hatred for America that will fuel terrorist ideology for decades to come. If his goal was to make America safe from terrorism, he has certainly chosen an odd path.

Every day brings more depressing news and images from Iraq which is now a quagmire by any definition of that word. Standing on the flight deck of the U.S. Naval ship in his Top Gun outfit with a "Mission Accomplished" banner displayed behind him is now just a cruel reminder that Mr. Bush was eerily and incredibly unaware that the mission had only just begun. And most depressing of all is the increasing evidence that we have asked our brave soldiers to fight for a questionable cause without providing enough support, enough equipment and enough manpower. As Robert McNamara ultimately learned, this is a tragic and indefensible road to disaster.

There is one critical difference between the Vietnam era and what is happening today. While returning soldiers from Vietnam often met an indifferent or even hostile response, the soldiers coming home from Iraq are being treated as the heroes they are. These are the people who have stepped up to pay for the price of freedom. They deserve better than this administration has given them. ❏

# Concord From Just Across the Acton Line

Concord is a cool July dawn as the mist rises from the fields along Monument Street. Quiet, no sounds but the air rushing past a bicycle helmet and the tires racing along pavement before anyone is awake.

Concord is the walking lady, sturdy strides along Harrington, backpack full but not over-full, face set and determined that there are miles to go today and more tomorrow.

Concord is a seat at Starbucks, a grande latte in hand, watching the parade of the coffee-challenged, noticing out in the parking lot how many sneak a left turn.

Concord is seven shivering children waving American flags in front of the West Concord 5 & 10 as the local Olympic hero rides by in a flatbed truck.

Concord is paddling back against the current from the Old North Bridge to the boat house, wishing the river would cut you a break.

Concord is a Friday night football game and the sparse home crowd realizing that this year's team is good, really good.

Concord is watching your 6-year old son answering the question of balance on his bike for the very first time; riding away wobbly but alone while you rub your lower back and feel your eyes mist up.

Concord is finishing 214th in the 5-mile Minuteman Run on July 4, happy to cross the finish line hand in hand with a special friend.

Concord is the rising sun over Mattison Field.

Concord is a smoked turkey sandwich with lettuce, tomato and mayonnaise on French bread at the West Concord Supermarket.

Concord is Doris and Richard Goodwin having breakfast at Friendly's on Thoreau Street.

Concord is discovering that your neighbors, a sweet elderly couple named Patterson, are the parents of the guy who writes bestselling murder mysteries like "Kiss the Girls."

Concord is surviving the Rt. 2 rotary without an accident for five years and wondering if it's worth contacting the Guinness Book.

Concord is the stream of people, many of color, walking a long, burdened walk from the train station down Commonwealth Avenue toward the prison for visiting hours.

Concord is explaining to every guest why a town such as Concord is home to a prison. As if we could take a vote and have it moved to Billerica.

Concord is a kava party at the Natural Gourmet.

Concord is befriending Debra Stark who can tell you what kava is.

Concord is Mike Curtis, the fiction editor of the Atlantic Monthly for 35 years, hitting an outlandish, no-look, running hook shot during Sunday afternoon pickup hoop games at the Hunt Rec Center.

Concord is secretly wishing you had a tri-cornered hat and britches so you could dress up and march in the Patriot's Day Parade.

Concord is debating the death penalty with Lorie on a morning run out to Route 2 and back. And never coming to agreement.

Concord is being a writer and strolling along Author's Ridge in the Sleepy Hollow cemetery on a cold December day, wondering where the beautiful words all go when they die.

Concord is tossing pitches to your 73-year old mom at the new ball field at Rideout and having her whistle a line drive past your ear.

Concord is Sal the barber who really sings in a barbershop quartet.

Concord is a skate on the black ice of Walden Pond on a February afternoon with only a lone ice fisherman off in the distance.

Concord is a friend who takes you to see the Dalai Lama while she searches for her elusive, life-sustaining center.

Concord is waiting for the black bears in the backyard and the light to change on Main Street.

Concord is countless generations and five-year sojourns; mansions on Monument, cottages on Cottage.

Concord never bends. It is in your soul, more than a town, just south of heaven. ❑

Printed in the United States
25348LVS00005B/85-108

9 780976 245308